PSYCHOLOGY
from a
CHRISTIAN
PERSPECTIVE

— SECOND EDITION —

Ronald L. Koteskey
Asbury College

UNIVERSITY
PRESS OF
AMERICA

Lanham • New York • London

Copyright © 1991 by

University Press of America®, Inc.
4720 Boston Way
Lanham, Maryland 20706

3 Henrietta Street
London WC2E 8LU England

First edition © 1980 by Abingdon Press

Library of Congress Cataloging-in-Publication Data

Koteskey, Ronald L., 1942-
Psychology from a Christian perspective /
Ronald L. Koteskey. — 2nd ed.
p. cm.
Includes bibliographical references and index.
1. Psychology and religion. 2. Christianity—Psychology.
3. Psychology. I. Title.
BF51.K68 1991
150.19—dc20 91-2424 CIP

ISBN 0–8191–8203–6 (alk. paper)

The paper used in this publication meets the minimum requirements of
American National Standard for Information Sciences—Permanence
of Paper for Printed Library Materials, ANSI Z39.48–1984.

Contents

Preface

The first edition of this book was basically a compilation of journal articles written to develop a Christian psychology. Of course, those articles were originally written for psychologists, but the book was widely used by college students in their first course in psychology.

In this revision, I have taken that readership into account. As I wrote, I tried to keep four "-tions" (pronounced "shuns") in mind. Those became my basic principles in completely rewriting the book. They were condensation, simplification, implication, and application.

Condensation meant that I shortened (condensed) the chapters. No chapter could be more than six pages. Although each chapter stands alone, it builds on previous chapters. I wrote each chapter to read with a corresponding chapter in a general psychology text, to put that chapter in a Christian perspective.

Simplification meant that I wrote more simply. Rather than writing for other psychologists, I wrote for freshmen in college or seniors in high school in their first course in psychology.

Implication meant that each chapter had a section on what the Christian faith implied about the psychological topic discussed in that chapter. Of course, with my self-imposed length limit, only a few implications could be presented in each chapter, but those served the purpose of showing that the Christian faith has something to say to psychology.

Application meant the each chapter had a section about how we could use the psychological principles discussed in the chapter in living Christian lives. Again, length limitations prevented many applications, but those presented showed that psychology has something to offer Christians.

I would like to thank Asbury College for granting me a one-quarter work leave during which the first draft of the book was written.

Chapter 1

A Christian Perspective

Psychology and Christianity have been in conflict during much of the twentieth century. In the first half, the dominant forces in American psychology clearly expressed their negative opinions about Christianity.

For example, on page two of his book *Behaviorism*, John Watson (1930) said that, like a voodoo doctor, "Christ had his magic; he turned the water into wine and raised the dead to life....Magic lives forever...tales get woven into the folk lore...get organized into religions...passed on as gospel."

Likewise, when writing a friend in 1927 about his forthcoming book on religion (*The Future of an Illusion*), Sigmund Freud said that the subject matter of the book was "my completely negative attitude to religion, in any form and however attenuated" (Schur, 1972, p. 403). Later in his preface to Part III of *Moses and Monotheism*, Freud noted that his work "reduces religion to a neurosis of humanity and explains its enormous power in the same way as a neurotic compulsion" (Schur, 1972, p. 469).

By mid-century the conflict had decreased and Christian psychologists were beginning to integrate psychology and Christianity. Roman Catholics founded the American Catholic Psychological Association in 1947, and Protestants founded the Christian Association for Psychological Studies in 1955. In 1965 graduate education integrating the two began with the doctoral program in clinical psychology at Fuller Theological Seminary. In 1975 Psychologists Interested in Religious Issues (PIRI) became a division of the American Psychological Association.

However, toward the end of the century, some Christians have begun to revive the controversy. In *The Seduction of Christianity*, Dave Hunt and T. A. McMahon (1985) said, "In the name of the latest psychology we are being led back into primitive paganism/shamanism" (p. 174). Continuing with the thesis that psychology is really sorcery, "psychologized shamanism," they said that "psychology is in the fullest sense a rival religion that can never be wedded to Christianity" (p. 191).

Martin and Deidre Bobgan (1987) became even more vehement in their attack on efforts to combine the two. They titled their book *Psychoheresy* and divided it into five parts, each with an inflammatory title:

"Psychoseduction," "Psychotheology," "Psychobabble," "Psychoquackery," and "The Psychological Way Or the Spiritual Way?"

The Seduction of Christianity remained at the top of the Christian best-seller list for months, and many Christians became convinced that they should stay away from psychology in any form.   Although Hunt and McMahon (1985) had much truth in their book, they went too far. They rejected all of psychology because of the error of some fringe groups. This is comparable to people rejecting Christianity because of the actions of some cults.

Hunt and McMahon pointed out that some people "interpret Scripture through a grid of mysticism blended with Jungian psychology" (p. 175). They were right. The problem is that those people have reversed what is the grid and what is to be interpreted.

I wrote this book to do just the opposite. I wrote it to reinterpret psychology from a Christian perspective. That is, I believe that Christianity is primary, "the grid," and I am interpreting psychology within that world-view.

I begin by presenting a Christian perspective and interpreting psychology as a whole within that perspective in the first two chapters. Then each following chapter places another part or several parts of psychology in it. By the end of the book all of psychology is reinterpreted in detail from that Christian perspective.

A Christian Perspective

To develop a Christian world-view, we need to begin at the beginning, with the opening words of the Bible: "In the beginning God created the heaven and the earth" (Genesis 1:1).   These ten words, translated into English today the same as they were nearly four centuries ago, give us the broad outline of a Christian perspective.

God

"In the beginning God..." (Genesis 1:1a) proclaims God the source of all in existence. He is independent of nature, infinite, supreme, and absolute. Nothing limits his sovereignty. He is subject to no laws or powers that transcend him. He is a personal being who is infinite in nature, distinct and separate from the universe which he created and which he sustains.

God reveals himself to us in several ways. One way is the Bible in which he spoke through individuals who recorded the history of Israel, the life of Jesus, and the story of the early church. He also reveals himself in his general (natural) revelation, through the world he created. Psalm 19 and Romans 1 tell us that God has revealed enough of himself in his creation to make his eternal power and divinity clear. In fact, even people who have not heard God's special revelation have no excuse not to know of him.

The World

"...created the heaven and the earth" (Genesis 1:1b) tells us that the world is the creation of God. It is neither identical with him nor a part of his being, but something he created and sustains. Since a moral, rational being made the world, it is real, he created it good, and it is orderly. Humans, made in God's image, can discover the patterns and regularities by examining the world he made.

Humans

"So God created man in his own image..." (Genesis 1:27a) tells us that we are created beings--like animals, plants or inorganic matter. In addition, it tells us that we are special--spiritual beings made in God's image. We are a unity of spirit and matter. Remembering that we are a unity, we may look at ourselves from different vantage points. Viewing ourselves from one point, we emphasize how we are like the rest of creation. Viewing ourselves from the other point, we emphasize how we are like God. Figure 1.1 shows a diagram of this perspective.

                         HUMAN
                         BEINGS
CREATED_____**IN THE**_____**IMAGE OF GOD**
LIKE ANIMALS_____**AS WELL AS**_____**LIKE GOD**

Figure 1.1. A Christian perspective.

Created--Like Animals. A little thought leads to the conclusion that humans are more like animals than like anything else in creation. We are more like animals than either inorganic creation or plants. We are finite beings, similar to animals in both body and behavior.

The Bible points out several times in Psalm 49 that we must die, like any animal. It also notes that both humans and animals breathe the same air, both die, both are made of the dust of the earth, and both must return to it (Ecclesiastes 3). Like the rest of creation, humans depend on God for everything, even their continued existence.

In the Image of God--Like God. God made us male and female in his own image. Although some people believe that the fall into sin erased that image, the Bible says that the image remains. When God prohibited murder, he said that to kill a human is to kill one made like himself--and that statement was made after the fall (Genesis 9).   The New Testament also notes that God made us all in his own likeness (James 3).

Although the Bible talks about the evil in people, it also talks about the good in them. Psalm 139 speaks of humans being wonderfully made. Psalm 8 says that God made humans only a little lower than himself. He crowned them with glory and honor and gave them dominion over his creation.

Implications--Definition

At this point you may ask, "What does all this have to do with psychology?" It is nice to have a Christian world-view, but, "So what?" What are the implications for psychology? All psychologists have world-views which influence what they think about psychology. Let us explore how the definition of psychology fits into our Christian perspective, a Christian world-view.

Psychologists today usually define psychology as the study of behavior and mental processes. The discipline began in the nineteenth century as the study of mental processes, during the first half of the twentieth century became the study of behavior, and finally during the last half of the century became the study of both. This definition, by the way, fits into our Christian perspective as shown in Figure 1.2.

Behavior

When concentrating on observable behavior, psychologists look at how humans are similar to animals. In fact, they often study behavior with the same tools they use to study animals. Furthermore, since humans are similar to animals, psychologists argue that the study of animal behavior has implications for the study of humans.

	HUMAN BEINGS	
CREATED	IN THE	IMAGE OF GOD
LIKE ANIMALS	AS WELL AS	LIKE GOD
Overt Behavior	DEFINITION	Mental Processes

Figure 1.2. The definition of psychology from a Christian perspective.

Mental Processes

When concentrating on mental processes, psychologists are really looking at how humans are similar to God. God said, "Come now, and let us reason together" (Isaiah 1), a mental process. We can reason with him because we are rational beings, created in his image.

One danger in using this schematic diagram of our Christian perspective is that we may see it as wrongly implying dualism, a division of ourselves into physical and mental components. We want instead to emphasize the unity of human beings. You may ask, "Are people really like animals or really like God? Should we study behavior or mental processes?" Those are inappropriate questions because they are rooted in a "dualistic" framework. Humans are both like animals *and* like God. We must study both behavior *and* mental processes. Psychologists have tried studying just one or the other, and they found that such an approach leads to an incomplete psychology of humans.

Application--Goals

You may also be asking, "What does all this have to do with Christianity?" It is nice to learn something about psychology, but, "How can I use this in my Christian life?" As our Christian beliefs have implications for psychology, so psychology has implications for our Christian lives. Let us explore how psychology's goals fit into our Christian perspective.

Different psychologists have different goals, depending on what they choose to do in psychology. However, these goals fit into two general categories, academic and applied. Figure 1.3 shows these goals in our Christian perspective.

CREATED	HUMAN BEINGS IN THE	IMAGE OF GOD
LIKE ANIMALS	AS WELL AS	LIKE GOD
Overt Behavior	**DEFINITION**	Mental Processes
Understand Creation	**GOALS**	**Make People God-Like**
(academic)		(applied)

Figure 1.3. Goals of psychology from a Christian perspective.

Academic

Some psychologists choose to make understanding God's creation their major goal. They apply this to both sides of the perspective. They want to describe, understand, and predict behavior and thinking. Such psychologists study anything that might have an influence on behavior and mental processes.

The study of the psychology of religion is all about using psychology to understand religious thinking and behavior. Such psychologists study such things as guilt, concepts of God, and changes in behavior following religious conversion. The Society for the Scientific Study of Religion specifically uses the methods of psychology and sociology to better understand religions of all kinds.

Applied

Other psychologists choose to apply their knowledge to change behavior and mental processes. They want to control how other people act and think. Control in this sense does not mean to manipulate, but to change for the better. They want to help students learn in school, to help people adjust to changes in their lives, and so forth.

As Christians, we specifically want to use our knowledge to help people become more like God. We want them to become more loving, more gracious, more merciful, more just, and so forth. Some ministers specialize in pastoral counseling to help people become more God-like. Seminaries and Christian colleges and universities have developed graduate programs integrating psychology and Christianity to educate Christian clinical psychologists to help people become more like God.

Chapter 2

Methods in Perspective

Chapter 1 stated a Christian perspective and showed how the definition and goals of psychology fit into it. This chapter places in that perspective both the methods psychologists use and the approaches they take to psychology.

Methods

To accomplish their goals, psychologists have developed a variety of methods. Some methods help reach academic goals, others the applied goals. Some are more appropriate for the animal-like aspects of humans, others for the God-like aspects. Figure 2.1 shows these methods in our Christian perspective.

	HUMAN BEINGS	
CREATED_____	IN THE_____	IMAGE OF GOD
LIKE ANIMALS_____	AS WELL AS_____	LIKE GOD
Overt Behavior	**DEFINITION**	Mental Processes
Understand Creation	**GOALS**	Make People God-Like
Experimental	**ACADEMIC METHODS**	**Descriptive**
Behavioral	**APPLIED METHODS**	**Cognitive**

Figure 2.1. Methods of psychology from a Christian perspective.

Academic Methods

Psychologists interested in describing, understanding, and predicting behavior have developed two major approaches to research. I call these the experimental method and the descriptive methods.

Experimental. Only the experimental method leads to cause-effect conclusions. As shown in Figure 2.1, this method is well-suited to studying the animal-like aspects of humans because it involves experimental control.

Although scientists usually present the experimental method as a relatively recent invention, it was used more than 2500 years ago by Daniel. In that experiment diet was the independent variable. The experimenter gave one group of students wine and rich food, and he gave the other group water and vegetables. Other than that he treated the two groups alike.

Health was the dependent variable. At the end of the study the group given water and vegetables looked healthier and better nourished. Thus, the experimenter concluded that water and vegetables were better for the students than wine and rich foods, so he changed their diets permanently (Daniel 1).

Descriptive. Although the experimental method is very good for finding causes of behavior, such control is not always possible. For example, in 1 Kings 18 both Elijah and the prophets of Baal tried to control what God did. Of course, God is sovereign, and no one can control what he does. In cases like this where we are dealing with the God-like aspects of people, we cannot control what God does. Thus, we must use some of the descriptive methods that psychologists have developed, as shown in Figure 2.1.

Psychologists interested in describing behavior often use observation, either in a natural setting or in the laboratory. They watch what people do and carefully describe the behavior. In 1 Kings the observer recorded the behavior of both Elijah and the prophets of Baal, the time of day, how many people participated, how many stones he used, and how much water they poured. Some psychologists increase the precision of their observations by giving tests or taking surveys with carefully worded questions. Others do case studies in which they study one person at a time in detail.

Psychologists interested in predicting behavior most often use the correlation method. By determining the relationship between two variables, they can use mathematical formulas to predict one from the other. For example, one can predict quite accurately how well students will do in school from their performance on intelligence tests.

Applied Methods

Psychologists whose goal is to change behavior and mental processes have developed several methods to do that as well. We can classify these methods as behavioral and cognitive ones, as shown in Figure 2.1.

Behavioral. Some people's primary interest is changing behavior. Industrial psychologists want to increase the output of workers. Probation officers want to see that people they are supervising do not commit crimes. Clinical psychologists want to get rid of abnormal symptoms in their patients. In all these cases, the primary goal is to change behavio.

Psychologists have methods that are effective in changing behavior. They first developed the methods on animals, and then found them to work well on humans. These methods usually involve giving rewards for desirable behavior and withholding those rewards when undesirable behavior occurs.

Cognitive. Other psychologists want to change mental processes. Educators want to help students think. Advertisers want to change how people perceive their products. Counseling psychologists want to change how clients feel about others in their families. The primary goal is to change mental processes--thoughts, perceptions, and emotions.

Psychologists have methods that change mental processes. Not surprisingly, most of these involve talking, a mental process itself. Educators carry on discussions in their classes to help students learn to think. Advertisers present words and images to alter perceptions. Therapists encourage clients to talk about things that are bothering them.

Of course, since human beings are a unity, it is often rather futile to try to change only one side of the diagram, either behavior or mental processes, without changing the other. In recent years, psychologists have emphasized changing both at the same time.

Approaches to Psychology

As psychology matured during the last century, several major approaches developed. These began as separate "schools," or systems, of psychology which emphasized different aspects of psychology. Today they are all part of psychology and fit into our Christian perspective as shown in Figure 2.2. We have already discussed two of these while talking about methods.

CREATED LIKE ANIMALS	HUMAN BEINGS IN THE AS WELL AS	IMAGE OF GOD LIKE GOD
Overt Behavior	**DEFINITION**	Mental Processes
Understand Creation	**GOALS**	Make People God-Like
Experimental	**ACADEMIC METHODS**	Descriptive
Behavioral	**APPLIED METHODS**	Cognitive
Behavioristic	**APPROACHES**	**Cognitive**
Biological	Psychoanalytic	**Humanistic**

Figure 2.2. Approaches to psychology from a Christian perspective.

Behavioristic

The behavioristic approach clearly falls on the animal-like side of our perspective. John Watson (1913/1968), founder of behaviorism, said in his first article about it that the behaviorist recognized "no dividing line between man and brute." Although most people taking the behavioristic approach today are not as radical as Watson, their emphasis is still on the animal-like aspects of humans.

Cognitive

Psychology began in Germany as the study of consciousness in a system later called structuralism. This, of course, was a study of a mental process.   A quarter-century later another school of psychology called Gestalt psychology arose. This system emphasized the study of perception and thinking, more mental processes.   Although these approaches were overshadowed by others in the United States during the first half of the twentieth century, the study of mental processes emerged during the last half in the form of cognitive psychology. The cognitive approach places an emphasis on the rational features of human beings. As such, it clearly falls on the God-like side of our Christian perspective in Figure 2.2.

Biological

Early psychologists often had degrees in physiology, and they frequently titled their early books *Physiological Psychology*, even though the content was more cognitive.   This biological background has become a major approach to psychology during the last half of the twentieth century. Physiologically humans are much like animals, so this approach to psychology clearly falls on the animal-like side of our perspective in Figure 2.2.

Humanistic

About mid-century several psychologists became concerned that some aspects of human beings were being ignored. Humanistic psychologists emphasized the dignity, worth, and full development of the potential of every person. They saw humans as being basically good, free, and creative. Humanists study all aspects of human experience, such as love, hate, fear, hope, humor, happiness, the meaning of life, and responsibility.   Thus, humanistic psychology fits into the Christian perspective on the God-like side in Figure 2.2.

Psychoanalysis

Psychoanalysis was one of the two major forces in psychology during the first half of the twentieth century. It developed in an applied rather than an academic setting, so most psychoanalysts were primarily interested in providing therapy for the disturbed. Psychoanalytic theory placed great emphasis on unconscious motivation, conflict, and symbolism.

Psychoanalysis does not fit clearly on either side of our Christian perspective. Some psychoanalysts place major emphasis on the unconscious, irrational id. Others place their emphasis on the rational ego which operates at the conscious, as well as the unconscious, level. Thus, this approach has both animal-like and God-like aspects of humans. To show this, I have placed it between the two columns in Figure 2.2.

Implications

Whether people are in academic or applied psychology, the perspective from which they view psychology will make a difference in what they do in psychology. I have found it to affect what I do in psychological research and what I think of psychology as being. Since personal values so influence this section, I am going to tell you how this has changed my behavior and thinking personally.

Methods

One way that viewing psychology from a Christian perspective changed what I do in psychology was in the choice of research problems. As an experimental psychologist, I began by doing research using rats and mice. While I still believe that research with animals has implications for humans, I became convinced that I should concentrate my research on more God-like aspects of humans. I now am doing research on the development of identity, including religious identity, particularly in adolescents.

Another way that viewing psychology from a Christian perspective changed what I do is in how I conduct research. Realizing that God made people in his image, I have made it a point not to use deception in my research. Although we may justify the use of deception in extreme circumstances, it has become far too routine in psychological research. I believe a Christian perspective should influence how we do our research as well as what we study.

Approaches

Placing the various approaches to psychology in a Christian

perspective helps me see their limitations and how they are related. For example, much of my training was from a behavioral point of view. A Christian perspective helped me realize that behaviorism is an incomplete psychology of human beings. However, rather than rejecting it because of its limitations, I see that it is a necessary part of a Christian psychology. If I ignore the similarity of humans to animals, I, too, will have an incomplete psychology.

Many psychologists have recognized the need to look at both aspects of humans, and tried to unite both sides of our perspective by combining two approaches. E. C. Tolman (1932) tried to unite Gestalt psychology and behaviorism into purposive behaviorism. Many psychologists today call themselves cognitive behaviorists. However, such attempts have such difficulty in combining opposites that they usually have to change one--into the other. Of course, from our perspective, we change both, resulting in a new unity.

Applications

We can apply both the methods and approaches to psychology in Christianity. Again I want to use personal examples.

Methods

When I became interested in identity, of course I looked at what the Bible had to say about it. However, when I wanted to develop a measure of identity to use with people today, I turned to the methods of psychology. I developed a number of statements that people could rate, then used the technique of factor analysis to develop the best identity scales possible with those statements.

Approaches

Christians use all the approaches presented in this chapter to help people who need therapy. We will elaborate these five approaches through-out the book as they come up again and again. Christians use techniques from the behavioristic, biological, psychoanalytic, cognitive, and humanistic approaches to help people become more like God. By the time you reach Chapter 16, you will be familiar with them, and you will see that every major approach to psychology has developed a therapy. Christians use at least some parts of all of these therapies.

Chapter 3

Biological Foundations

Psychology lies between the natural and social sciences, between biology on the one hand and sociology on the other. In this chapter we begin with the subject matter that is the most like biology. Then we will proceed throughout the book toward that most like sociology.

Physiological Psychology

Physiological psychology attempts to explain behavior and mental processes in terms of anatomy and physiology. Whenever behavior takes place, certain physiological events occur. For the leg to jerk when someone taps the patellar tendon, receptors in the muscles must begin an impulse in a neuron leading to the spinal cord. This neuron must initiate an impulse in a neuron leading to the leg muscle, which must contract. Changes in these receptors, neurons, and muscles will change behavior.

	HUMAN BEINGS	
CREATED	**IN THE**	**IMAGE OF GOD**
LIKE ANIMALS	**AS WELL AS**	**LIKE GOD**
Overt Behavior	**DEFINITION**	Mental Processes
Understand Creation	**GOALS**	Make People God-Like
Experimental	**ACADEMIC METHODS**	Descriptive
Behavioral	**APPLIED METHODS**	Cognitive
Behavioristic	**APPROACHES**	Cognitive
Biological	Psychoanalytic	Humanistic
Physiological	**STRUCTURE**	

Figure 3.1. Physiological psychology from a Christian perspective.

Likewise, physiological events occur during mental processes. The electrical activity in the brain changes as a person moves from deep sleep, to dreaming, to light sleep, to relaxed wakefulness, to concentrating on a problem. People familiar with brain-wave patterns can tell much about a person's mental processes by looking at the tracings on paper.

Although some Christians do not like to admit it, humans are very similar to animals physiologically. As we saw in Chapter 1, the Bible says that both humans and animals "are of the dust" and "have the same breath" (Ecclesiastes 3). Today we would say that God made both of atoms and both need oxygen. Since we are so similar to animals biologically, physiological psychology is on the animal-like side of our perspective in Figure 3.1.

Humans are so much like animals that physicians sometimes use animal parts for humans. For example, surgeons often use valves from pig hearts to repair human hearts and skin from pigs to help burn victims heal. Although they could make many comparisons, physiological psychologists have concentrated on the nervous system and the endocrine system because those systems have the most influence on behavior and mental processes.

Nervous System

From our Christian perspective we are grateful for what physiological psychologists are learning about the relationship of the nervous system to behavior and mental processes. We all know people whose behavior and thinking have changed as a result of strokes, brain tumors, concussions, and damage due to hardening of the arteries in the brain.

Since the human nervous system is basically very similar to the nervous system of other mammals, much of the data gathered in physiological psychology is from animals. Scientists can often then generalize to humans. They work with animals for obvious ethical reasons. Damage to neurons in the brain and spinal cord is permanent, so scientists cannot arbitrarily injure these tissues to see the effect on human behavior and thinking.

Physiological psychologists also study the effects of events at the synapses, the places where information passes from neuron to neuron. Again, as Christians, this pleases us because we all know people whose behavior and thinking have changed as they used psychoactive drugs. These drugs, whether legal (such as tranquilizers or antidepressants) or illegal (such as cocaine or LSD), change how neurons communicate. Knowing what is happening at the synapse may enable psychologists to help those who use drugs.

Endocrine System

Humans are also similar to animals in the hormones secreted by their endocrine glands. In fact, some of the hormones people take are from animal tissue. The circulatory system carries these chemicals to all parts of the body where they have a specific effect on a particular part of the body. They control how large we grow, our energy level (behavior), and affect neural transmission (mental processes), among other things.

Implications--Spiritual Psychology

While physiological psychology fits well on the animal-like side of our perspective, there is nothing in contemporary general psychology to fit on the God-like side. Humans have muscles, nerves and glands like animals, but they are also spiritual beings like God. This fits into our Christian perspective as shown in Figure 3.2.

CREATED LIKE ANIMALS	HUMAN BEINGS IN THE AS WELL AS	IMAGE OF GOD LIKE GOD
Overt Behavior	DEFINITION	Mental Processes
Understand Creation	GOALS	Make People God-Like
Experimental	ACADEMIC METHODS	Descriptive
Behavioral	APPLIED METHODS	Cognitive
Behavioristic	APPROACHES	Cognitive
Biological	Psychoanalytic	Humanistic
Physiological	STRUCTURE	Spiritual

Figure 3.2. Spiritual psychology from a Christian perspective.

Although humans are similar to animals in many ways, when dealing with such phenomena as language, personality, creativity, morality, and ethics, we need to look more to comparisons with God than to the structure and function of the brain or glands. God is spirit, and humans created in his image are also spiritual beings.

When Jesus talked with the woman at the well in Samaria, he emphasized that God is spirit and that those who worship him must do so in spirit and in truth (John 4). The apostle Paul notes that God is spirit, and in the next sentence he notes that the spirit of the Lord himself changes us into God's likeness (2 Corinthians 3). Many other passages of Scripture refer to the fact that humans are spiritual beings.

If we are to look at the God-like aspects of humans, we need to know what God is like. Of course, we cannot know all about God, but he has chosen to reveal certain things about himself. We call these his attributes. A. W. Tozer (1961) wrote about them in The Knowledge of the Holy, which he subtitled, "The Attributes of God: Their Meaning in the Christian Life." We will use his list here.

Some people are reluctant to compare humans with God. They believe there is such a great difference between the two that we cannot make comparisons. This is true for what Schaeffer (1968) calls the infinite aspects. As we look at Tozer's list, we find that more than half of them are related to God's infinite aspects. We cannot be like him in these ways: only he is self-existent, self-sufficient, eternal, infinite, immutable, omniscient, omnipotent, transcendent, omnipresent, and sovereign.

Meaningful comparisons can be made on other attributes. Remember that the Bible itself, God's own special revelation to us, repeatedly makes these comparisons. It tells us to be holy, perfect, loving, and merciful. Let us now consider the remaining nine attributes of God listed by Tozer, attributes in which we find ourselves like God.

A Trinity. He is three persons in one God, a unity. God is a social being, and so are we. God is also a unity, and we must emphasize the unity in our social relationships.

Wise. He is a God of wisdom, a wisdom we in our finiteness cannot understand. Although we cannot have perfect wisdom, he encourages us to seek wisdom, and he promises to give it to us.

Faithful. God does not break his promises. He also encourages us to keep our vows. With God's help, it is possible to keep our covenant with him.

Good. We define goodness by the very nature of God himself. We are to be like him, good not only to our friends, but to our enemies as well.

Just. God is no respecter of persons. He treats everyone fairly. We are to be fair to those under our authority, as he is just to us.

Merciful. God is actively compassionate. His justice does not stop his mercy. God specifically commands us to be merciful as he is merciful.

Full of Grace. His grace enables him to help the undeserving, to spare the guilty. We are to forgive others as Christ forgave us. Jesus even taught us to pray that in "The Lord's Prayer."

Love. God's very nature is to love. Jesus said that he had loved us as the father had loved him and that we were to continue in his love. He commanded us to love one another as he had loved us.

Holy. God is absolutely holy, and in his presence we are aware of our lack of holiness. In both the Old and New Testaments God tells us to be holy because he is holy.

Finally, insights from scripture shed light on concepts used by psychologists. For example, those taking the psychoanalytic approach believe that the conscience part of the superego develops at about the time a child starts to attend school. Romans 2 talks about Gentiles not having the law, but doing "by nature" what the law requires. It says they have the law "written on their hearts." This conscience, a basic sense of right and wrong, is innate. Of course, the specific things considered right and wrong may change as a person matures, but the basic sense of justice is part of the image of God in humans.

Applications

Some of the findings of physiological psychology have implications for us as Christians. Meyer (1975) pointed out that research shows that the right and left sides of our brains seem to function differently, as though we have "two minds." In most people the left side of the brain is verbal and analytic while the right is spatial and intuitive.

If we are to worship God with our whole mind, we must worship him in both the intricate, rational discourses of the book of Romans and the mystical, "visual" experiences of Ezekiel. We must worship him both in the logic of the words of the hymns and in the beauty of the music to which we sing them. As we minister to others, we must minister to both the rational and the intuitive aspects of their humanity.

Since people are physical and spiritual, problems can develop on either the animal-like side or the God-like side or both sides of our perspective. Thus, treatment should be relevant to the source of the problem.

Physiological Treatments

As we have seen, people can have disorders in their behavior or mental processes because of physiological problems. Knowing the source of the problem may tell us how to treat it, if it is treatable. Damage to neurons in the brain and spinal cord is permanent, and any recovery usually means learning to do the same things using different neurons.

People may lose their capacity to think clearly and their speech may become slurred because of syphilis, an infectious disease. In this case, a massive dose of penicillin will stop the deterioration. They may become anxious and irritable, lose memory, and have hallucinations because of a lack of the vitamin niacin. Putting them on a high-protein diet rich in vitamins brings improvement.

Disorders of the endocrine glands can also cause changes in behavior and thinking. People with too little hormone from the thyroid gland in their neck become sluggish, sleep much of the time, and have little motivation. Those who have too little hormone from the adrenal cortex become depressed, anxious and withdrawn. Increasing these hormones cures the problem.

Spiritual Treatment

Since humans are spiritual beings, a possible disorder is sin. Sin is primarily a matter of transgressing against God, sometimes by offending another person, one made in God's image. Sin, of course, results in guilt and guilt feelings which motivate the person to want to do something about the guilt.

If the problem is sin, the only real solution is forgiveness. Many people try to get rid of the guilt feelings without taking care of the guilt problem itself. They can solve the sin problem only through confession, repentance, and faith in Christ. Treatment through counseling or with drugs will not get at the root of the problem and will bring only temporary relief.

Interaction

Since people are a unity, problems on one side of our perspective may cause problems on the other, or they may have problems on both sides. People with a hormone deficiency (a physical problem) may pray for energy. When that energy does not come, they may lose their faith in God (a spiritual problem). People who become drunk (a spiritual problem) repeatedly may become addicted to the alcohol (a physical problem). This combination of problems becomes increasingly difficult to solve.

ter 4

ent

Developmental _____ ___ udy the changes in behavior and mental processes resultin_ _____ _turation and experience. During the first half of the twentieth c__ _y such psychologists spent most of their time studying development in childhood and adolescence. However, more recently they have studied development throughout life.

CREATED	HUMAN BEINGS IN THE	IMAGE OF GOD
LIKE ANIMALS	AS WELL AS	LIKE GOD
Overt Behavior	DEFINITION	Mental Processes
Understand Creation	GOALS	Make People God-Like
Experimental	ACADEMIC METHODS	Descriptive
Behavioral	APPLIED METHODS	Cognitive
Behavioristic	APPROACHES	Cognitive
Biological	Psychoanalytic	Humanistic
Physiological	STRUCTURE	Spiritual
Immaturity	DEVELOPMENT	**Maturity**

Figure 4.1. Developmental psychology from a Christian perspective.

Developmental psychology fits into our Christian perspective as shown in Figure 4.1. Note that infants are more animal-like. They do not yet have language or make moral choices. As people mature, they become more God-like, or at least they have that potential. Psychologists studying development in different areas have repeatedly found that people progress from animal-like to God-like.

Cognitive Development

The leading developmental psychologist emphasizing cognitive development was Jean Piaget (1973). According to him, as individuals mature, they gain new ways of thinking about old problems. People progress through several stages as their mental processes develop.

Sensorimotor

During the first two years of life, infants discover how their actions influence things around them. They learn how to reach for some things and how to push others away. However, as the name of the stage implies, they are "thinking" with their senses and motor responses. Animals can apparently do as much.

Preoperational

During the next five years of life children learn to use language, but still have difficulty understanding that things can look different to other people. They classify objects by a single dimension, such as color or shape. By comparison, animals cannot use language, but they can react to objects along a single dimension.

Concrete Operational

During the next five years children begin to classify objects along several dimensions. They also can think logically about objects, but only when the objects are physically present. Their mental processes have become much less like animals.

Formal Operational

Finally, at about the age of puberty, people are able to think logically and abstractly, like other adults. They can test hypotheses systematically and think about hypothetical problems.

Note the progression from sensory-motor (animal-like), reflexive movements to the beginnings of language to the ability to think and reason abstractly (God-like). Figure 4.2 shows this change, along with changes in moral development to be discussed next.

Moral Development

Although Piaget studied moral judgment in children, it was Kohlberg's (1973) work which sparked the interest of American psychologists. Kohlberg found that moral development continued into adulthood.

Most people know about his first six stages of moral development, organized into three levels.

Animal-like_____**God-like**

Sensorimotor   COGNITIVE DEVELOPMENT Formal Operational
Preconventional   MORAL DEVELOPMENT   Postconventional

Figure 4.2. Cognitive and moral development in Christian perspective.

Preconventional Level

    In early stages, children are quite animal-like in their moral behavior.   During Stage 1, the punishment orientation, the physical consequences of an action determine whether it is right or wrong for the child. Infants, like animals, avoid punishment. During Stage 2, the reward orientation, children obey to get rewards, just as animals do.

Conventional Level

    Older children become less animal-like in their moral judgments. In Stage 3, the good-boy/good-girl orientation, children conform to what others expect so people will think they are "good."   In Stage 4, the authority orientation, they obey the rules just because the rules exist. They believe everyone ought to obey the law, even if the law is wrong. Many people never move beyond this level.

Postconventional Level

    At about the age of puberty, some people begin thinking in larger terms.   During Stage 5, the social-contract orientation, they act on ideas thought to be good for the general welfare. Finally, during Stage 6, the ethical principle orientation, they act on self-chosen ethical principles. They do something because it is right rather than because it avoids punishment, gets reward, brings acclaim, is against the law, or is for everyone's good.

    Nearly everyone who discusses Kohlberg lists the previous stages, but Kohlberg (1973) also proposed a stage 7. In this stage, the ontological-religious orientation, people take on a cosmic perspective. They identify with an infinite perspective and value life from that standpoint. People sense the unity of the whole, and they feel like a part of that unity. From our Christian perspective, we would say that the person becomes more God-like.

    Again, looking at Figure 4.2, one can see that moral development proceeds from animal-like to God-like. Animals can respond for reward or to avoid punishment. No animal is going to be a martyr for a cause it believes is right. Humans, however, can be like God in that respect.

Psychosocial Development

Erikson (1963) modified and extended Freud's psychoanalytic theory. He believed that development continued throughout life, and revolved around a series of psychosocial crises. People can become more or less like God at each crisis, as shown in Figure 4.3.

When discussing spiritual topics, such as guilt and sin, it hardly makes sense to put "animal-like" on the left side of our diagram, so I have labeled it "unlike God." However, it still makes sense to put God-like on the right side. Erikson lists the favorable outcomes at each stage of development as including hope, willpower, purpose, competence, fidelity, love, care, and wisdom--all God-like characteristics.

Before leaving the psychoanalysts, we should mention the order in which Freud believed the structures of personality developed. When infants were born, they had only ids, the animal-like, evil, instinctual part of personality. The next structure to develop was the ego, the rational part of personality. The final structure to develop was the superego, the moral part of personality. Again notice the progression from being unlike God to like God as the person develops.

Unlike God_____Like God

PSYCHOSOCIAL DEVELOPMENT

mistrust	trust
doubt	autonomy
guilt	initiative
inferiority	industry
confusion	identity
isolation	intimacy
self-absorption	generativity
despair	integrity

Sin   SPIRITUAL DEVELOPMENT   Glorification

Figure 4.3. Psychosocial and spiritual development in Christian perspective.

Implications

A Christian world-view has implications for development. The Bible refs to Christians as "babes in Christ" or as mature. This view also gives us the goal toward which development is proceeding.

Spiritual Development

Most theologians do not use the term "stages" to talk about spiritual development, but Berkhof (1946) refers to "stages in the work of redemption" (p. 536). Although there is little agreement on the specifics of these stages, most theologians agree there are four general stages of development toward God-likeness.

Sin. Humans are born in a sinful state, commonly called "original sin." This is the root of the overt sins appearing later in life. Humans can do nothing to rescue themselves from this sinful state, a state very unlike God, as shown in Figure 4.3.

Salvation. We often classify people who have asked God for forgiveness and been justified by God as "born again," or saved. With sins forgiven, they are now living and growing in Christ. They are becoming more God-like.

Sanctification. Theologians probably disagree about this stage of development more than any other. They disagree about when it takes place and what happens in it. Some say it is completed during life, others at death, still others after death. Some emphasize its aspect of dedication to God, while others emphasize its aspect of transformation or being made holy. Whatever the emphasis, in sanctification people become even more like God.

Glorification. The final general stage is glorification. This means life in heaven where people are even more like God. As the Bible puts it, "we shall be like him for we shall see him as he is" (1 John 3).

Goal of Development

Psychologists have talked about us being in the process of becoming, but what we are becoming is not always clear. We are just "becoming" (Allport, 1955) or "actualizing" (Maslow, 1968; Rogers, 1959). Such people say we are realizing our potential, but they are not clear about the nature of that potential. From our Christian perspective we can say that our potential is to become like God. Of course, most of us are more comfortable with saying we want to be Christ-like, but he was like God.

Death

During the second half of the twentieth century psychologists have become interested in death and dying. They see these as a part of our development. From a secular perspective, death is the end, as Kubler-Ross (1975) titled her book, *Death, the Final Stage of Growth.*

However, from our perspective, while we do see death as a stage in development, it is not the final one. Christians also look forward to the resurrection. Our hope is not that doctors will find some new cure to keep our animal-like bodies functioning a little longer, but that God will resurrect our bodies and make us even more like Christ. Resurrection, not death, is the final stage of development. Of course, development may continue in eternity, but we know little about that.

Application

We can apply the findings of developmental psychology to our treatment of others as well as our own behavior and mental processes. The findings about cognitive and moral development should have an effect on what we expect relative to these areas in others.

Cognitive Expectations

When trying to teach others about God, we must be careful not to expect them to understand beyond their level of cognitive development. Children have difficulty understanding concepts about the Holy Spirit. God came concretely in the person of Christ, "God with skin on" as some say. Even small children can understand about Jesus. Those a little older can understand about "God the father." They have parents and can think of God as a parent.

However, even when dealing with adolescents and adults, we must remember that not everyone is able to think abstractly. Many people never reach the stage of formal operations. If they have trouble understanding algebra, we must not expect them to have the same kind of understanding of religious concepts that someone in the stage of formal operations has.

Moral Expectations

Likewise, we must not expect moral choices above the level that people are able to make. Infants respond on the basis of reward and punishment, and it makes little sense to talk with a two-year-old about a social contract with humanity. As Kohlberg found, even many adults remain at the level of keeping rules. They may not be able to think in terms of doing to others as they would want others to do to them.

Chapter 5

Sensation

  Since the discipline began, psychologists have studied how humans come into contact with their environment and become aware of the world around them. In the first system of psychology, at the end of the nineteenth century, the most basic element was sensation. During the first half of the twentieth century behaviorists studied the connection between the stimulus (sensation) and the response.

  Sensation is the study of how we change the physical energy in our environment into neural impulses received by the brain. Through sensation we have contact with the world which God created. Beyond the traditional five senses of vision, hearing, taste, smell, and touch, psychologists study others, such as senses in the muscles, the joints, and the inner ear.

CREATED_____ LIKE ANIMALS_____	HUMAN BEINGS IN THE_____ AS WELL AS_____	IMAGE OF GOD LIKE GOD
Overt Behavior	**DEFINITION**	Mental Processes
Understand Creation	**GOALS**	Make People God-Like
Experimental	**ACADEMIC METHODS**	Descriptive
Behavioral	**APPLIED METHODS**	Cognitive
Behavioristic	**APPROACHES**	Cognitive
Biological	Psychoanalytic	Humanistic
Physiological	**STRUCTURE**	Spiritual
Immaturity	**DEVELOPMENT**	Maturity
Sensation	**AWARENESS**	

Figure 5.1. Sensation from a Christian perspective.

Sensation is an animal-like attribute of humans, as shown in Figure 5.1. Primarily concerned with physical energy and how that energy becomes neural impulses, sensation appears in the same column as the other parts of psychology that study the animal-like aspects of persons.

This is the first of three chapters in which we will consider how persons become aware of their environment, so we will call the general category "awareness." Most psychologists consider vision and hearing the most important senses, so they have spent most of their time studying these two.

Vision

Structure

Our eyes are very much like those of animals. Even primitive animals have the same basic plan--that of a lens forming an image on a set of receptors. Human eyes are typical of vertebrates. To reach the receptors, light passes through the cornea, the aqueous humor, the lens, and the vitreous humor to reach the retina, which lies "inside out." As in most vertebrates, light passes through blood vessels, nerve fibers, and nerve cells to get to the rods and cones.

Human eyes function much like those of animals. Pigments absorb the light energy which breaks them down. The rods of both humans and other vertebrates contain rhodopsin and give sensations of black and white. The cones of both contain iodopsin and give sensations of color.

The neural pathway to the brain is similar in both humans and other mammals. Impulses beginning on the nasal side of each eye cross and go to the opposite side of the brain. Those beginning on the temporal side of each eye do not cross but go to the same side of the brain.

Sensitivity

The sensitivity of human eyes is similar to that of animals. Humans are sensitive to about the same range of light as animals. Of course, cats and other nocturnal animals can see in dimmer light because of a reflective coating on the back of their retinas, but the general range is about the same. If an animal has both rods and cones, its dark adaptation is very much like that of humans. If the animal is colorblind (has no cones), its adaptation is much like that of human rod vision. If the animal has only cones (poor night vision), its adaptation is similar to that found in human cone vision.

Human vision is very similar to that of animals. Whether we consider anatomy, physiology, neural pathways, or sensitivity, human eyes are like animal eyes. We find much the same in our sense of hearing.

Hearing

Structure

Our ears are anatomically very similar to those of animals. Of course, the appearance of our outer ear is quite different from that of animals, but the outer parts of human ears have little to do with hearing. The middle and inner ear are very similar in both humans and animals. The eardrum gathers the vibrations of the sound waves and sends them through the tiny bones of the middle ear to the inner ear.

The cochlea, containing the receptors for hearing, is very similar in humans and animals. Both have a membrane containing receptors moving up and down. When those receptors bend, they start impulses in the neurons synapsing with them. Human ears function much like those of animals. Investigators using the ear of a cat as a microphone discovered the cochlear microphonic. Human ears also produce the cochlear microphonic.

The neural pathway to the brain is similar in both. It is more complicated than that for vision, but the crossing and recrossing on the way to the brain is much the same.

Sensitivity

The sensitivity of the human ear is similar to that of animals. Humans and animals hear about the same range of pitches. Of course, some animals, such as cats and dogs, can hear higher pitched sounds than humans because the bones in their middle ears are smaller and can vibrate faster. When you blow a dog whistle, your dog can hear it, but you cannot. However, the overall range is still remarkably similar.

Humans and animals hear about the same range of loudnesses. Again, some animals may be able to hear softer sounds because of slight differences in their ears, but the overall range is similar. As with vision, whether we are talking about anatomy, function, or sensitivity, humans and animals are remarkably similar.

Other Senses

Although psychologists have not studied the other senses as extensively, humans are similar to animals in them as well.

Taste

We experience four basic tastes: sweet, salt, sour, and bitter. For some time psychologists thought there might be four types of taste cells, one sensitive to each taste. However, recordings in single nerve fibers of the cat showed that it is not cell differences, but the pattern of neural impulses which gives taste quality.

Smell

Since it is so difficult to do research on smell (the receptors are way up inside the nose) psychologists have used animals. Of course, again some animals, such as bloodhounds, have a much better sense of smell than humans (although their eyes are much worse). However, in general humans and animals are very similar regarding the sense of smell.

Touch

Our sense of touch includes warmth, cold, pressure, and pain. The parts of the body served by each of the spinal nerves are remarkably similar in animals and humans. In fact, Leukel (1976) shows the boundaries in humans in a four-legged position and interprets that as evidence that these boundaries evolved before animals (and humans) walked upright.

We do not often receive conscious sensations from the senses in our muscles, joints, and inner ears. However, like the other senses, these are similar in humans and animals.

Implications

Although we are primarily like animals in our senses, we must remember that we are also like God. Because our senses are our means of contact with the world around us, they may be the way Satan tempts us. Let us consider examples from the Bible of people tempted through their senses.

The Fall into sin as described in Genesis 3 involved vision. When Eve looked at the fruit, it was "pleasant to the eyes." This led to her taking and eating it--and the Fall. When Achan saw a beautiful robe, some silver, and some gold, it led to coveting and stealing (Joshua 7). When David saw Bathsheba taking a bath, it led to lust, adultery, and murder (2 Samuel 11).

Today the senses can lead to temptation, as they did thousands of years ago. Of course, we have different ways of appealing to the senses now, but the principles are the same. Let us consider a few examples.

Vision

Television, movies, and full color printing can lead to the same sins we found in the Old Testament. As Achan began to covet what he saw, so does advertising lead to coveting today. The ads portray many different material goods, and people just "have to have" them, even though many goods advertised are totally unnecessary. As David was led into lust through what he saw, so are people today through X-rated movies, videos, and magazines.

Hearing

The same kinds of temptations can come to us through our ears. Advertising on the radio can make us want things. Although people have expressed much concern about sex and violence on television, they have complained less about what disk jockeys play on radio. Constantly playing in our homes, automobiles, and places of business, many of these songs are about illicit sex and violence.

Taste and Smell

These two senses are related because they are both chemical senses. They are most commonly associated with eating, and can lead to gluttony. Even when we are not hungry, the smell of food can make us suddenly want it, as anyone knows from walking past a restaurant or bakery. When eating, how much we eat often depends more on how the food tastes than on how much we need.

Touch

The sense of touch can lead to sex outside marriage. Petting has become an expected part of courtship. It is a normal part of events leading to sexual intercourse. However, when unmarried couples try to bring about sexual arousal through petting but stop before going on to intercourse, they often fail to stop.

Application

Most people are aware that they can damage their eyes by looking directly at too bright a light. They do not look directly at the sun. However, the same people may damage their ears by listening to very loud noises. Damage to hair cells in the ear is permanent, and it has become popular for Christian teens to listen to loud noises.

Less than two hours of exposure to a 100-decibel noise, such as a concert by Christian musicians, results in some hearing loss. The ringing in your ears after such a concert indicates damage. Although some of the hearing comes back, other loss is permanent. Such loss is cumulative; it keeps adding up through life.

Even less obvious is the damage that is caused in the same way by stereo headphones. In this case, even the person standing next to you may not realize that you are damaging your ears permanently by playing loud music. Studies show that more than half of college students have some form of hearing impairment.

Chapter 6

Perception

Perception begins where sensation leaves off. Perception is the process of organizing and interpreting our sensations. One text says it "gives meaning" to our sensations through an "active process" (Crooks & Stein, 1988). Another calls perception "an active mental process" (Myers, 1989). Since perception is a mental process giving meaning, it is obviously on the God-like side of our Christian perspective in Figure 6.1.

	HUMAN BEINGS	
CREATED	**IN THE**	**IMAGE OF GOD**
LIKE ANIMALS	**AS WELL AS**	**LIKE GOD**
Overt Behavior	**DEFINITION**	Mental Processes
Understand Creation	**GOALS**	Make People God-Like
Experimental	**ACADEMIC METHODS**	Descriptive
Behavioral	**APPLIED METHODS**	Cognitive
Behavioristic	**APPROACHES**	Cognitive
Biological	Psychoanalytic	Humanistic
Physiological	**STRUCTURE**	Spiritual
Immaturity	**DEVELOPMENT**	Maturity
Sensation	**AWARENESS**	**Perception**

Figure 6.1. Perception from a Christian perspective.

Although perception is on the God-like side of our perspective, we must not forget that people are a unity and that perception has close ties with the animal-like side as well. Of course, it is related to sensations because it organizes them. It takes the jumble of sensations and makes them into a meaningful experience.

It is also related to physiological psychology. In fact, Hubel and

Wiesel (1979) received a Nobel Prize for showing the relationship between the two. Some neurons respond when a horizontal line appears on the retina. Others respond to a vertical line. Still others respond to lines of different angles. Higher level neurons respond to lines meeting at given angles. Hubel and Wiesel called these neurons "feature detectors" because they respond to particular complex features in the environment.

Let us now consider some of the major perceptual phenomena and how our God-like mental processes solve the problem each presents.

Depth Perception

When an object moves across the field of vision, it is rather easy to see that a person can directly interpret where it is by its position on the retina. That is, if the object is off to the left, its image will fall on the right side of the retina. Likewise if it off to the right, the image will fall on the left side of the retina. However, the problem is not so simple in depth perception. How can people see a three-dimensional world when they have only two-dimensional retinas?

Monocular Cues

They can use input from only one eye to begin to see depth. For example, as an object gets larger on the retina, people see it as being nearer. If one object blocks out part of another, people see the first as being closer. If the air is hazy or foggy, people see more distinct objects as being nearer. The more they have to strain to focus the object on the retina, the nearer people perceive the object to be. They can use their God-like mental processes to draw conclusions from these, and other, cues from one eye to tell how far away an object is.

Binocular Cues

Since most people have two eyes, they can integrate the input from both to tell how far away something is. The more the eyes have to cross to keep the image on the fovea of each retina, the nearer people perceive the object to be. Since the eyes are a few inches apart, the image on each retina is slightly different. People compare these differences using their God-like mental processes and draw conclusions about which objects are nearer and which are farther away.

Depth perception is the mental process in which people take input from their eyes and give it meaning relative to distance. They take input from two-dimensional retinas, organize it, and interpret it in three-dimensional terms.

Constancies

Whenever an object changes position in the field of vision, sensations change, but people see the object remaining the same. Constancy is being able to see a stable world in the face of changing sensations.

Shape Constancy

When standing directly in front of a door, its image on the retina is a rectangle. However, as the door opens, the image becomes a trapezoid, and finally just a line as the door fully opens. However, the person watching it open sees the door itself as keeping the same rectangular shape. Psychologists call this mental process "shape constancy."

Size Constancy

When a car approaches us, its image on our retina becomes larger and larger. However, as we saw earlier, people interpret this change in the size of the image as a difference in distance, not a difference in size. Because we have God-like mental process to interpret our sensations, we can see objects as either changing in size (as in blowing up a balloon) or changing in distance (as in a ball coming toward us).

The same is true in other areas as well. Sun glasses change the color and brightness of the sensations. However, through color constancy and brightness constancy, people can still tell red lights from green lights and drive safely.

Illusions

Sometimes people make objects so that others will misinterpret them. Using their active mental processes, people draw wrong conclusions from the sensations they receive. Psychologists explain the two common illusions shown in Figure 6.2 in this way.

Ponzo Illusion   Muller-Lyer Illusion

Figure 6.2. Illustrations of two illusions.

Ponzo Illusion

Although both horizontal lines in the Ponzo illusion are exactly the same length, the top one looks longer to most people. Apparently, this is because their mental processes interpret the other lines as being "parallel" and receding in the distance, like railroad tracks. Since the top line seems to be farther away, it looks like it is longer.

Muller-Lyer Illusion

Although both horizontal lines in the Muller-Lyer illusion are exactly the same length, the one on the bottom looks longer to most people. Apparently this is because, as in the Ponzo illusion, people interpret the one on the bottom as being farther away (like the corner of a room). Since the one on the bottom seems to be farther away, it looks like it is longer.

Psychologists have made many figures to mislead this God-like mental process of drawing conclusions from sensations, but in the natural world, those conclusions are nearly always correct.

Implications--Extrasensory Perception

The question of whether or not people can have perceptions without sensation has been hotly debated in psychology, and in Christianity, for many years. Since researchers have not developed reliably repeatable demonstrations or experiments, some scientists doubt that it is possible. Since people have occasionally classified extrasensory perception with the occult, some Christians believe it is evil. However, since God created humans in his image, it might be possible for them to have perceptions without sensation--extrasensory perception.

Telepathy

Telepathy is the transfer of thought from one mind to another without ordinary sensory channels, such as talking, writing, or signals of any kind. As Christians, we certainly believe this is possible in the form of prayer, direct communication between our minds and God. God hears prayers too deep for us to express in words (Romans 8). Because we are like him, we communicate with him telepathically.

Clairvoyance

Clairvoyance is the perception of an object or event without using the known senses. At times in the Bible, people were aware of physical objects without using their senses. Moses was aware of water in the desert twice when there was no sensory indication of its presence (Exodus 17, Numbers 20). Christians today are sometimes aware of another person needing prayer in difficult situations.

Precognition

Precognition is the perception of a future event. In Christianity this is occasionally called prophecy. Some of the prophecies made in the Old Testament came about in the New. For example, the second chapter of the New Testament contains the fulfillment of three specific prophecies of the Old Testament. Others were fulfilled later, and some are still to be fulfilled in the future.

Although it is not perception, people often include psychokinesis with the three kinds of extrasensory perception. Psychokinesis is the manipulation of objects without using any known physical force. Answers to prayer are often in the form of bringing about changes in the environment, so people may well have psychokinetic capacities.

The previous sections show that we have extrasensory capacities, at least when God is involved. The Bible is not clear about whether or not we have telepathy, clairvoyance or precognition without special intervention by God, but it does leave that possibility open. In eternity, we will be even more like God, and we may have full extrasensory capability.

Applications

As Christians, we can apply the study of perception beyond the laboratory. How we perceive the world and ourselves plays a major part in our adjustment.

Defense Mechanisms

Students of general psychology often study lists of defense mechanisms. Professors tell students that everyone uses these defenses, and that their use is fine as long as people do not carry them to an extreme. However, this is a case where we must be careful about what we take from psychology to apply to Christianity.

Projection involves seeing our own shortcomings or unacceptable impulses in others. The late 1980s gave us some classic examples of projection. Evangelists who preached the most about the lust they saw in other people had a problem with pornography themselves.

Rationalization involves giving "logical" reasons for our behavior. Rather than thinking of themselves as selfish, other "Christians" spent millions of dollars on themselves. They said they did it because God's people deserved the best, and they were God's people.

Denial, refusing to acknowledge reality, is probably the most primitive defense mechanism. John said that when we deny our sinfulness, we deceive ourselves. Denial and the other defense mechanisms all involve self-deception. We must not forget that they involve changing our perception, but do not change objective reality. In fact, they may make us more comfortable and keep us from working to change the real problem in ourselves.

Psychotherapy

While we do not want to defend against reality by deceiving ourselves, neither do we want people to maintain wrong perceptions of themselves and others. Psychologists often use psychotherapy to change perception.

Some Christians have wrong perceptions of themselves. Even though forgiven, such people may see themselves as quite different from what they would like to be. By being accepting and nonjudgmental, we can help others change their perceptions of themselves. They can come to see themselves as more Christ-like, as they really are. Of course, this works only if they are already the kind of Christian they would like to be.

Some Christians have wrong perceptions of others. They may see even other Christians as being against them when they are not. Some seem to be always fighting a battle even in church because they have mistaken what other people are trying to do. We need to help them change their perceptions of others.

Chapter 7

Consciousness

Psychology began as the study of the contents of consciousness. During the first half of the twentieth century psychology abandoned the study of consciousness as being unscientific, but returned to its study during the last half of the century.

Of course, consciousness is what we are aware of at the moment. It includes perceptions, thoughts, memories, and feelings. Since consciousness is a mental state, it appears on the God-like side of our Christian perspective in Figure 7.1. From its definition, consciousness obviously belongs with other topics on that God-like side of our perspective.

	HUMAN BEINGS	
CREATED_____	**IN THE**_____	**IMAGE OF GOD**
LIKE ANIMALS_____	**AS WELL AS**_____	**LIKE GOD**
Overt Behavior	**DEFINITION**	Mental Processes
Understand Creation	**GOALS**	Make People God-Like
Experimental	**ACADEMIC METHODS**	Descriptive
Behavioral	**APPLIED METHODS**	Cognitive
Behavioristic	**APPROACHES**	Cognitive
Biological	Psychoanalytic	Humanistic
Physiological	**STRUCTURE**	Spiritual
Immaturity	**DEVELOPMENT**	Maturity
Sensation	**AWARENESS**	Perception
		Consciousness

Figure 7.1. Consciousness from a Christian perspective.

Since humans are a unity, consciousness is also related to topics on the animal-like side of our perspective. People are conscious of their sensations and have memories of their childhood. Changes in physiology bring changes in consciousness. In fact, that is one of the largest problems in our society today, the effect of drugs on both mental processes and behavior.

Drugs

Since ancient times people have smoked, sniffed and swallowed chemicals to change consciousness. Today alcohol, tobacco, and caffeine are legal and widely used in our culture to alter it. Cocaine and marijuana are illegal and less widely used. Since psychologists are interested in the effects of drugs on consciousness, they classify such drugs relative to their effects on the central nervous system.

Stimulants

Stimulants increase the excitability of neurons in the central nervous system. Many people use caffeine, a mildly addicting cortical stimulant, to get a "lift." Tobacco smoke acts as an addicting stimulant to the sympathetic nervous system and makes people feel good. Cocaine is another central nervous system stimulant that influences mood. Many people in our culture want the increased awareness that comes from stimulants.

Depressants

Depressants decrease activity in the central nervous system. Alcohol is the most widely used depressant in our society. Some people take barbiturates regularly to bring on sleep. Others use heroin to get a feeling of well-being. These drugs are addicting and can be dangerous. If a person takes too much of a depressant, activity in the nervous system slows so much that it may stop.

Hallucinogens

Hallucinogens disorganize the activity of the central nervous system to cause distorted perceptions. The most widely used hallucinogen is marijuana. A chemist discovered LSD in the 1940s, which many used in the 1960s; although people used it less in the 1970s, it appears to be coming back. These drugs alter perceptions, especially those of space and time.

From our perspective, our goal is to become more like God. Although Christians disagree about the use of stimulants and depressants, few drugs make people more like God. God is love, but people under the influences of drugs are less aware of people around them, less merciful and compassionate. God is a rational being who invites us to reason with him, but people under the influence of drugs become less rational and lose touch with reality.

Sleep and Dreaming

Sleep and dreaming are also states of consciousness closely related to physiology. Brain wave patterns change as people fall deeper and deeper into sleep or as they dream. All of us experience these changes in consciousness.

When people say they go to sleep, they mean that they lose consciousness. Sleep is a loss of awareness. Studies of the activity of the brain, however, show that people go through regular cycles during a night's sleep. At some times the brain waves resemble wakefulness, and at others they are much larger and much slower.

People also go through periods when their eyes move rapidly. When awakened during those times, they often report vivid dreams. Dreams are a series of thoughts, "perceptions," emotions, and so forth taking place while a person is asleep, not consciously responding to the environment. Thus, dreams are mental processes which fit on the right side of our perspective.

Meditation

Although people have meditated for centuries, scientists did not become involved in studying meditation until the last half of the twentieth century. When Wallace & Benson (1972) showed that transcendental meditation (a state of consciousness) had physiological effects, psychologists became interested in it.

Transcendental Meditation grew rapidly after it began in the United states in 1958. The goal of meditators is to lose their individuality in pure Being, abstract being. They reach this goal by repeating a secret mantra for twenty minutes each morning and evening. This leads to a state of consciousness without any specific objects or subjects. The meditator tries to go beyond all thought to a state of pure awareness.

Transcendental Meditation is on the God-like side of our perspective. Of course, it is a state of consciousness, but even more than that, it is an expression of a religion (Hinduism) and applies to the spiritual aspect of humans. Although its proponents argue that it is not a religion, both the US District Court and the US Court of Appeals have ruled that it is. Thus, no one can teach it in public schools. Of course, as Christians, we should avoid practicing another religion.

Hypnosis

Hypnosis is a heightened state of suggestibility. People have made so many claims for hypnosis that it is difficult to separate fact from fiction.

People have claimed to use it to relieve pain, stop smoking, be better athletes, help their memory, and regress in age.

Whatever the facts finally turn out to be, hypnosis is a mental process that goes on the God-like side of our perspective. Many have called it an altered state of consciousness. Hilgard (1986) concluded that hypnosis is a divided consciousness. That is, one part of a person's consciousness is totally unaware of what is going on around the person. However, another part, the "hidden observer," knows what is happening and can report on it.

Whether hypnosis is an altered state of consciousness or a divided state of consciousness, it still is a mental process that is on the God-like side of our perspective.

Near Death Experiences

Since Moody's (1976) popular book about the experiences of people who have been close to dying, many people have reported these near-death experiences. Most of the experiences are positive, often including going through a tunnel toward a bright light and feeling a warm spirit.

Are these visions? Are they hallucinations? Are they the actual way to heaven? No one knows, and people have proposed all of the above as explanations. Some maintain that this phenomenon shows that God will ultimately save everyone, because even bad people go toward the light. Others caution that Satan himself masquerades as an angel of light (2 Corinthians 11). Whatever the explanation, these experiences are on the God-like side of our perspective.

Implications

Visions

Visions are similar to dreams, except that people experiencing them are awake and aware of what is happening. Visions are states of consciousness that have been a part of the Christian faith from its beginning. In both Old and New Testaments God spoke to his people through visions.

Old Testament. God seemed to use visions at major turning points in the history the Jews. He appeared to Abram in a vision to promise him a son when Abram thought he would have none (Genesis 15). God spoke to Jacob in a vision to tell him not to be afraid to go to Egypt (Genesis 46).

New Testament. God also used visions at turning points in the early history of the Christian church. He used a vision to send Ananias to see Saul who, up to that time, had been persecuting Christians. Saul himself had just experienced a vision of Jesus (Acts 9). When God was trying to convince the apostles that he included the Gentiles in Christianity, he used a vision to get Cornelius to send for Peter. Then he used a vision to enlighten Peter concerning the Gentiles (Acts 10).

Why So Different? When Ezekiel saw the Lord, he talked about a whirlwind, a cloud, a fire and four indescribable creatures, as well as wheels and rings (Ezekiel 1). When John saw a vision of Jesus on Patmos, he described Jesus as like fire and his feet like brass (Revelation 1). Both of these men also reported hearing noises along with their visions.

We may ask why these experiences sound so different from normal reality. It is probably because they are trying to describe something for which no words exist. To get some idea of what this must be like, pretend you are visiting a two-dimensional world and trying to explain what the third dimension is like. Abbott (1884/1952) did this in *Flatland*. By reading that, one can get some idea of what it would be like to try to describe something when the language just does not have the words.

Hallucinations? Some of the visions recorded in the Bible sound like the hallucinations of the mentally ill. How can one tell the difference? There are probably two factors to consider. First, is the vision consistent with God's revelation in scripture? God will not contradict himself. Second, what is the behavior of the person having the vision like otherwise? If the person has other symptoms of mental illness, such as delusions, the "vision" may well be an hallucination.

Dreams

Remember that God spoke to his people in dreams as well as visions. God used dreams at crucial times in Israel's history in the Old Testament. Again, in the New Testament God used dreams at the beginning of the Christian faith. In the prophecy of God's pouring out his spirit on humanity, Joel noted that some would have dreams and others would see visions. We must not dismiss all our dreams as the effects of something we have eaten. God speaks through dreams at times.

Applications

What psychologists have learned about these states of consciousness have applications in our Christian lives. Let us now look at some of them.

Drugs

Of course, nearly every community has a campaign to keep people off street drugs, but what about the legal, socially acceptable drugs? How does a person decide whether or not to use caffeine, tobacco, alcohol, or tranquilizers? The Bible does not deal with any of these except alcohol, and it only says not to be drunk with that. Here are two general principles to follow.

First, as Christians we are not to be under the control of anything, and all the above drugs are potentially addicting. If you begin to become addicted, get off the drug immediately. To check whether you are becoming addicted, go without it for a week to see if you can function comfortably and normally. If not, stop taking the drug completely until your nervous system readapts.

Second, do not use drugs that harm your body. As more and more research comes in, psychologists are finding more about the effects of these drugs. Most of them do harm us (and our unborn children when pregnant women take them), and we should not use them.

Meditation

Psychologists have found benefits to meditators. Meditators feel relaxed, peaceful, and less anxious. Meditating lowers blood pressure, decreases drug use, and increases scores related to mental health and self-esteem on tests. These benefits are available to Christians, but not through Transcendental Meditation.

The Christian goal in meditation is not lack of awareness, but concentration on God and his Word. Christian meditation is consciousness filled with an awareness of God himself, not nothingness. A Bible study on meditation shows how different Christian meditation is.

Chapter 8

Learning

This chapter begins a three-chapter section about the intellectual aspects of humans. Since learning is a mental process, it might appear on the God-like side of our perspective. However, rather than defining it in terms of knowledge, as many people do, psychologists define learning as a relatively permanent change in behavior as a result of experience. Since learning refers to behavior, I have placed it on the animal-like side of our perspective in Figure 8.1.

	HUMAN BEINGS	
CREATED	**IN THE**	**IMAGE OF GOD**
LIKE ANIMALS	**AS WELL AS**	**LIKE GOD**
Overt Behavior	**DEFINITION**	Mental Processes
Understand Creation	**GOALS**	Make People God-Like
Experimental	**ACADEMIC METHODS**	Descriptive
Behavioral	**APPLIED METHODS**	Cognitive
Behavioristic	**APPROACHES**	Cognitive
Biological	Psychoanalytic	Humanistic
Physiological	**STRUCTURE**	Spiritual
Immaturity	**DEVELOPMENT**	Maturity
Sensation	**AWARENESS**	Perception Consciousness
Learning	**INTELLECT**	

Figure 8.1. Learning from a Christian perspective.

Not only does it fit there by definition, but psychologists have also studied learning primarily with animals. It began with the study of learning in dogs at about the turn of the century, and then it expanded to mostly rats and pigeons by the middle of the century. Psychologists have spent most of their time studying two kinds of learning, classical and operant conditioning.

Classical Conditioning

Ivan Pavlov (1927/1960) first studied Classical conditioning early in the century. In classical conditioning, psychologists pair a neutral stimulus with a stimulus that causes a response. The neutral stimulus soon elicits the response itself. In Pavlov's original experiments with dogs he rang a bell (a neutral stimulus) just before he gave food (which would, of course, bring a response). At first the dogs salivated only to the food. However, after several pairings, the dogs also salivated to the bell.

Humans, like animals, learn by classical conditioning. Suppose a psychologist always sounds a tone just before she blows a puff of air in a person's eye. The person will soon blink to the sound of the tone. Suppose parents always say, "No!" just before slapping a child's hand as it reaches for a vase. The child will soon withdraw the hand and cry at the word, "No!" Classical conditioning clearly fits on the animal-like side of our perspective.

Sometimes classically conditioned responses are misunderstood. If people feel guilty with a pounding heart during an invitation hymn in several church services, the heart rate (caused by guilt) may become conditioned to the hymn itself. Later these people may have the same heart rate when they hear the hymn, even after God has forgiven them. Not realizing that the heart rate is just an animal-like, conditioned responses, these people may think they are still unforgiven and question their salvation.

Operant Conditioning

B. F. Skinner (1938) first studied operant conditioning. In operant conditioning, behavior increases when psychologists follow it with a reinforcement. If the behavior does not occur, the psychologist gives no reinforcement. Skinner first studied this by giving food when a rat pressed a lever or when a pigeon pecked at a disk. The behavior of pressing or pecking increased as food was given again and again.

Humans, like animals, usually repeat rewarded responses. Children rewarded with M&M's for urinating will try to urinate again. People often reinforce each other's operant behavior. For example, when parents pick up a crying child, it stops crying. By doing this, the parents make the child more likely to cry because they rewarded its crying behavior by picking it up. The child makes the parents even more likely to pick it up again because it rewarded them for picking it up by stopping crying. Operant conditioning also would fall on the animal-like side of our perspective.

Religious behaviors can be the result of operant conditioning. When people feel less guilty because they put money in the offering, they become more likely to put it in again. If reading the Bible makes them feel better, they are likely to read it again. Rather than these being means of grace, they become animal-like operant conditioned responses.

Reinforcement and Punishment

Most psychologists deal with reward and punishment in terms of changing behavior. Outcomes tend to control behavior. People usually repeat rewarded responses and stop punished responses. This treatment is logical since learning is defined in terms of behavior, and on the animal-like side of our perspective.

Humans, like animals, respond to changes in reward and punishment. The larger the reward, the greater the response. The longer the delay of reward, the less learning. Even their patterns of responding to different schedules of reinforcement are remarkably similar.

When placed on a fixed interval schedule of reinforcement, one in which psychologists give reward after a given amount of time passes, animals soon respond with a "scalloped curve." This means that right after a reinforcement they stop responding. Then they gradually increase it until they are responding very rapidly at the time of the next reinforcement. This pattern repeats itself at every reinforcement. When placed on a variable interval schedule of reinforcement, one in which reward is given after random amounts of time, they respond at a steady rate.

Most students can illustrate that humans react the same way to these schedules of reinforcement by looking at their studying in two types of courses. They can keep track of the time they spend studying (study responses) in courses where teachers give grades only on the basis of tests every two weeks (fixed interval schedule). This results in a scalloped curve in which they do little, if any, studying right after they take a test, but cram most of the night just before the next test. They can compare this with courses in which teachers give pop quizzes (variable interval schedule). This schedule produces a constant rate of studying, just like in animals.

Cognitive Learning

As we must not forget the animal-like aspects when considering the God-like aspects of humans, so we must not forget the God-like aspects when concentrating on the animal-like. Learning is no exception. Early behaviorists repeatedly tried to explain learning without reference to cognition.

However, as Morris (1988, p. 202) puts it, "It would appear that, at least in the case of humans, there's often more to learning than meets the eye." Gestalt psychologists and those influenced by them have talked about insight, even in higher animals, since World War I (Kohler, 1925/1959). By the late 1960s, most psychologists realized that humans were God-like cognitive beings.

Albert Bandura (1971, 1986) proposed that individuals learn through observing others. Following this observational learning, people model their behavior after what they have seen.   Bandura first called his a "social learning theory," (1971) and he now calls it a "social cognitive theory" (1986).   What he is doing is calling attention to the God-like aspects of humans.

Implications

Psychologists have used their knowledge about learning, reward and punishment to increase productivity in the workplace.   As Christians, however, we must also remember that God made people in his image, and we must consider reward and punishment in terms of justice as well.

When deciding how much to pay a worker, we should think about more than how much we have to pay to get maximum production.   We have to consider what is a fair wage in that society for the work done.   We should neither pay people too little for the work they have done to maximize our profits, nor pay them more than they deserve.

Likewise, we should view punishment in terms of justice.   C. S. Lewis (1949/1970) took this position in his indictment of "the humanitarian theory of punishment" so prevalent today.   This theory views criminals as sick and in need of a cure, usually through psychotherapy.   There is no concept that we punish people because they deserve it.   This approach actually implies a low view of humanity, a view on the level of animals. To be punished because they deserve it makes people responsible beings created in God's image.   Although efforts at rehabilitation are right and good, they must not replace just discipline.

Applications

Since humans learn through classical and operant conditioning, we can use these to change behavior.   That humans are animal-like in this way is disturbing to some Christians.   However, that fact does not bother those looking at psychology from our Christian perspective.   They realize that while humans are like animals in some ways, this does not mean they are not like God in others.

James Dobson (1970) encouraged Christian parents to use reward to change the behavior of their children.   Because Dobson used some techniques of behaviorism, Adams (1973) erroneously called his system a Godless behaviorism.   Adams was reluctant to admit that humans could be animal-like in any way.

Classical Conditioning

Psychologists usually use the techniques of classical conditioning to change a person's emotional responses (likes, dislikes, fears) in order to change overt behaviors. The basic idea is that a person has learned unsuitable responses to some stimuli, so he must learn more suitable ones. The person can either extinguish the unsuitable response or learn an incompatible one.

A Christian whose heart still pounds during an invitation hymn will find that it pounds less and less the more he hears the hymn. The pounding heart was not a sign of guilt, but a classically conditioned response. It was a learning problem, not a spiritual one. It needed extinction, not forgiveness. Of course, a pounding heart may be a sign of real guilt, and then the person needs spiritual help.

Christians who had a cruel father may react negatively to the concept of "God the father." They need to forgive their fathers and, through healing of those memories, replace the hurt with love. Through classical conditioning the emotional responses on the animal-like side become less and less, and the Spirit gives help on the God-like side.

Operant Conditioning

Psychologists usually use techniques involving operant conditioning to directly change overt behavior. If people have rewarded inappropriate responses in the past, they must stop those rewards so the behaviors will be extinguished. The parent who does not pick up the crying child has stopped rewarding crying. If the parents have rewarded the child much in the past, the crying may go on for a long time, but it will get less and less over time.

Sunday school teachers may find using a token economy helps them maintain discipline in their classroom so their pupils can learn about God. In a token economy, people give rewards for specified behaviors. For example, teachers may reward children who refuse to sit still for staying in their chairs for five minutes at first, then for longer and longer times later. They may reward those who forget their Bibles for bringing them.

We must be careful in our use of reward and punishment. The response just given is the one rewarded or punished. For example, suppose a child has misbehaved and comes to confess his "crime." If the parents punish the child on the spot, they may suppress the behavior just done (confessing). The child will be less likely to confess in the future.

Chapter 9

Thinking

Thinking is the capacity to represent objects or events internally and to operate on these representations. Thinking is, even for psychologists, a mental process, so it appears on the God-like side of our perspective in Figure 9.1.

CREATED LIKE ANIMALS	HUMAN BEINGS IN THE AS WELL AS	IMAGE OF GOD LIKE GOD
Overt Behavior	**DEFINITION**	Mental Processes
Understand Creation	**GOALS**	Make People God-Like
Experimental	**ACADEMIC METHODS**	Descriptive
Behavioral	**APPLIED METHODS**	Cognitive
Behavioristic	**APPROACHES**	Cognitive
Biological	Psychoanalytic	Humanistic
Physiological	**STRUCTURE**	Spiritual
Immaturity	**DEVELOPMENT**	Maturity
Sensation	**AWARENESS**	Perception
		Consciousness
Learning	**INTELLECT**	**Thinking**

Figure 9.1. Thinking from a Christian perspective.

Language

The greatest challenge to placing the cognitive processes on the God-like side of our perspective has come in the area of language. Since the early twentieth century psychologists have tried to teach human language to other primates, but they have had little success. Chimpanzees learned to speak three or four words, but that was all, even when reared like human children.

Between 1950 and 1975 psychologists tried to teach apes to use sign language, and the results seemed quite impressive. Chimpanzees could learn a "vocabulary" of several hundred "words." From both the popular press and scientific literature it seemed that any day psychologists would make a breakthrough and carry on intelligent conversations with animals.

However, we must consider what makes up a language. Most linguists consider that a language has at least phonemes, morphemes, semantics, and syntax.

Phonemes and Morphemes

All spoken languages contain a number of basic sounds, phonemes. Probably no language has more than 80 phonemes, and English has only about 40. Phonemes are not meaningful, and animals can certainly make many of the sounds used in human speech.

The smallest unit of meaning in a language is a morpheme, usually made of two or more phonemes. Some morphemes are words, and others are prefixes or suffixes. The English language has about 50,000 morphemes. Animals can also make many of these sounds.

Semantics

Semantics is a system of rules that help us determine the meaning of words and sentences. For example, if I add the morpheme "ed" to the morpheme "laugh" it changes the meaning to something that happened in the past. Semantics includes the capacity to use "names" correctly, and animals have this capacity. Your dog can respond appropriately to your commands, whether spoken or signed. If phonemes, morphemes, and semantics were all there is to language, animals would have language capacity.

Syntax

The final requirement of a language is syntax, the rules for putting words together. People learn many of these rules without even thinking about them, but other rules take years of the study of grammar in school. Even a child knows that "I kicked the dog small" is incorrect English syntax. In English, adjectives ordinarily come before the nouns they modify, although this is not so in Spanish syntax.

During the early 1970s it seemed that animals could master syntax. However, Limber (1977) carefully studied the combinations of signs children and chimpanzees had used. He concluded that before the age of four all children produce new correctly structured complex sentences, but "there is little evidence that any ape ever did" (p. 284).

About the same time, Terrace (1979) set out to prove that chimps could learn a language. He named his chimp "Nim Chimsky," a sarcastic reference to linguist Noam Chomsky, and gave Nim the educational advantages of such things as Sesame Street. Rather than proving that chimps could use language, Nim changed Terrace's mind.

If we define a language as including being able to learn the rules of grammar as a part of language, animals cannot use language. Language is a God-like aspect of humans.

Thought

Thinking takes place through the use of concepts and images. Concepts are categories of things, not simply individual cases. Most of our knowledge is in the form of concepts, such as "car," rather than specific items, such as "the red 1961 Ford Falcon owned by Ron Koteskey." Mental images are scenes, sounds, or other "perceptions" we manipulate in logical fashion. When I described my car above, you may have "seen" an image of it or "heard" it running.

The study of this God-like capacity to form mental images was a part of psychology at its beginning more than a century ago. The first system of psychology, structuralism, maintained that consciousness consisted of sensations (Chapter 5), images, and affective states (Chapter 12). Although psychologists abandoned the study of images during much of the first half of the century, images have come back into psychology through the cognitive revolution.

God certainly encourages thinking. God is wise, and he encourages us to seek wisdom and understanding. One of the major themes of the book of Proverbs is to seek these. From our perspective, we would say that as we get these, we become more like God.

Problem Solving and Creativity

When people have a goal but no way to reach it, they are facing a problem. When we speak of a creative solution to that problem, we look for one that is both original and worthwhile. Psychologists have long studied problem solving and creativity.

God is the Creator and humans, made in his image, show creativity as well. Five times during creation (Genesis 1) God said, "It is good." Thus, the Bible indicates that he had made something original and evaluated it as worthwhile. Of course, God is self-sufficient and creates out of nothing, while humans work with what is already in existence and change its form.

Although many psychologists have ignored creativity, Maslow (1968) discussed it as a quality of self-actualizing people. He found it an inherent part of human nature, although the creative potential was often lost or buried. From our Christian perspective we also see it in all humans, a part of God's image in them.

Implications

Around the turn of the century, most psychology textbooks contained chapters on "will" or "volition." These chapters usually came near the end of the text because psychologists saw them as the major integrating process between thought and action. However, the concept of will came into disrepute in psychology. By mid-century one rarely found the word "will" in the index of most general psychology texts.

The two major forces in psychology, behaviorism and psychoanalysis, both saw humans as "being controlled" rather than "controlling." They believed that either our environment or unconscious internal forces controlled everything humans did. Rollo May (1969) finally broke the silence on will when he titled his book *Love and Will*.

From our Christian perspective we must reaffirm that people actually have the God-like capacity to make choices. We must also hold them responsible for the choices they make. God told his people to choose whom they would serve (Joshua 24), and Jesus said that he came that we might be free (John 8). As beings made in God's image, we actually have the power to choose.

Although the words "will" and "volition" have not returned to psychology, the concept is beginning to come back. Several texts now have sections on "decision making."

Applications

Although God made people cognitive beings in his image, their thinking is not always correct. They may have incorrect concepts, even about the Christian faith.

Faulty Concepts

People may have incorrect concepts about God. Some think of God as a hostile being keeping a record of all their wrong actions, just waiting to punish them. They ask, "Why is God doing this to me?" in times of sickness or accident. Others think of God as capricious. Youth may worry about not finding God's will for their lives in choosing a vocation or marriage partner. Their concept of God is of a person who makes them guess what he wants them to do, and punishes them if they cannot figure it out.

People may have incorrect concepts about humans, others made in God's image. Some look at the problem of overpopulation and talk about "people pollution." Rather than thinking of people as pollution, God thought they were important enough to send his son to die for them. Others expect absolute perfection out of church members. Paul addressed his first letter to the Corinthian church to "those called to be saints," but even a quick reading of that letter shows that the church had much room for improvement.

Cognitive Therapy

Beck (1976) proposed that psychological problems result from faulty learning and drawing incorrect conclusions. From this he developed cognitive therapy, an approach that aims at correcting wrong concepts. People may think, "If I made a mistake, it means that I'm inept." A cognitive therapist works with patients to help them see that they are drawing wrong conclusions. Patients discuss their assumptions, beliefs, and expectations, then come up with a plan to change their way of thinking.

Rational Living

Although much of his work is not acceptable to Christians, Ellis (1958) began his approach with an emphasis on the God-like aspects of people. He first called it "rational psychotherapy," founded the Institute for Rational Living, the Institute for Advanced Study in Rational Psychotherapy, and the journal, *Rational Living*. He believes that people become disturbed, not as a result of objective events in their lives, but as a result of the irrational beliefs they use to interpret these events. For example, if a person believes, "Everyone should love me for everything I do," that person will fail and may become emotionally disturbed.

Problem Solving

Christians face problems as individuals, as families, and as larger groups, such as churches. In their study, psychologists have developed more efficient methods of problem solving, and these are useful at home or church. When faced with a problem, people should be sure they understand the problem, generate possible solutions, evaluate the solutions, and apply the solution to their problem.

Difficulties can arise at any of the above steps. One particular problem in families or churches may be groupthink. Irving Janis (1972) found that in tightly knit groups, members may be slow to criticize a solution suggested by the group's leader. Anyone who questions the solution may be ostracized or accused of not having enough faith. As a result, such groups may come to poor solutions for the problems they face.

Chapter 10

Memory

Memory is the last chapter dealing with the intellectual processes. During the first half of the twentieth century psychologists viewed memory as a camcorder which recorded experiences that could be played back later. This implied that memory was passive and did not discriminate. If that were so, we would have to place it on the animal-like side of our perspective.

CREATED LIKE ANIMALS	HUMAN BEINGS IN THE AS WELL AS	IMAGE OF GOD LIKE GOD
Overt Behavior	**DEFINITION**	Mental Processes
Understand Creation	**GOALS**	Make People God-Like
Experimental	**ACADEMIC METHODS**	Descriptive
Behavioral	**APPLIED METHODS**	Cognitive
Behavioristic	**APPROACHES**	Cognitive
Biological	Psychoanalytic	Humanistic
Physiological	**STRUCTURE**	Spiritual
Immaturity	**DEVELOPMENT**	Maturity
Sensation	**AWARENESS**	Perception Consciousness
Learning	**INTELLECT**	Thinking **Memory**

Figure 10.1. Memory from a Christian perspective.

Unlikely as it may seem, a machine led to the idea that memory is an active, discriminating process. With the invention of the computer and the rise of information processing, psychologists began to think of the mind as an information processor. Thus, memory is now viewed as a mental process, on the God-like side of our perspective in Figure 10.1.

Of course, we must also remember that God created humans like he created animals. Memories are probably stored in the nervous system, and damage to it may change those memories. In addition, chemicals which change the functioning of the nervous system may change memories.

Three Processes

What gets stored in memory is not an exact replica of experience. As the eye is not a camera nor the ear a microphone, so the mind is not a camcorder. Psychologists now believe three processes occur in memory.

Encoding

Encoding is the process of perceiving an event and changing it into some form we can easily store. People shape, or categorize, or organize the information to fit their way of thinking. This encoding is an active, God-like, mental process, not a passive recording. Even though two people observe the same event, they may remember quite different things about it because they encoded it differently.

Storage

Storage is the process by which people keep the encoded information for future use. How much people can store and how long it lasts in memory depends on how they encode it. They can encode it to last a few seconds, or a lifetime.

Retrieval

The final process in remembering is retrieval. People use retrieval to bring encoded and stored information back to consciousness. Some current demand reclaims the information using the cues put on it when the person encoded it.

Three Systems

People apparently have three memory systems allowing them to code, store, and recall information. These three systems have different capacities and retain the information for different lengths of time.

Sensory Memory

Information comes through the senses and enters the sensory

memory. This memory has a relatively large capacity, but lasts for a very short time. While looking at a page in a book, a person can see the whole page, but the information leaves the sensory memory in less than a second. While listening to something, the information is available for several seconds.

Even in this first system of memory, mental processes come into play. Information in the sensory memory disappears unless people actively do something to retain it. At this stage people must pay attention. They selectively look, listen, smell, taste, or feel and give meaning to the information coming in. If not, they lose it. That is, to get the information to the second system, God-like mental processes are necessary.

Short-Term Memory

What people are thinking about at the moment is short-term memory, roughly the same as "consciousness." Items attended to in sensory memory come into short-term memory. This memory holds less than sensory memory, but it lasts longer. Short-term memory can hold only five to ten items. If more are put in, they push out items already there. Short-term memory lasts only a matter of seconds, perhaps thirty seconds at the most.

Unless people intervene with an intentional, God-like, mental process, they will lose these items. However, they can keep items in short-term memory by rehearsing, by repeating the information over and over. Of course, a few seconds after they stop rehearsing, they lose the material.

To get the information to the next system of memory, more God-like mental processes are necessary. At this point coding is necessary. The material must be changed into a form that will allow it to become associated with items already in memory. Some people have a subjective organization, and they recode the new information to fit. Others recode the information into images and store the images. Still others use mnemonic devices to code information. In seconds they forget material not encoded or rehearsed.

Long-Term Memory

Long-term memory is just that, long-term. Material remains in it for minutes, hours, days, years--perhaps a lifetime. In addition, it apparently has an unlimited capacity. It can never get so full that there is not room for more. Of course, information in it is coded, elaborated, and organized by God-like mental processes.

People may "forget" information in long-term memory because of interference as new material is put in. They may also "forget" if the correct retrieval cue is not present. That is, the information is there, but they cannot pull it out. Students often report this during, and just after, tests. As soon as they look at their notes to get a cue, it all comes back--too late.

Finally, people have to decode the information recalled, and during decoding they may change many details. People usually remember the basic facts about past events, but may disagree violently about the details. While decoding what they have stored, they use their God-like mental processes to fill in the details of what "must have happened."

Implications

God tells us to remember some things and to forget others. God gives us some ways to remember, and Christians have developed ways to "forget."

In Remembrance of Me

As Jesus celebrated his last Passover with the disciples, he told them to do it "in remembrance of me." The bread was to help them remember his body broken for them. The wine was to help them remember his blood given for them. This "last supper" has become the sacrament of communion, the eucharist, the liturgy or the mass observed by Christians everywhere. The command to observe it was a command to remember.

The Christian faith has other symbols as well to help Christians remember the fundamentals of the faith. The cross has become one of the central symbols of the faith, and appears repeatedly inside and outside churches. Cathedrals are even built in the shape of the cross.

Healing of Memories

Memories torment some people. People would like to forget experiences they had many years ago, but are unable to do so. The emotion attached to these memories causes intense suffering. Linn and Linn (1974) list six steps to healing of these memories.

Thank. Thank God for the gifts he gives. See yourself as created in God's image and thank him for making you.

Ask. Ask God what he wants to heal in you. Your goal is to become more like Christ, not only to experience fewer tensions or live up to what someone expects of you.

Share. Share the painful memory with Christ. Go back to the memory of the original event. Rather than focussing on the immediate problem of depression, mistrust, or impatience, go back in memory to where it started.

Forgive. Forgive those involved in the painful memory, unconditionally--as God would forgive them. God-like forgiveness does not depend on the other person changing and becoming worthy. Such forgiveness begins to replace the hurt with love.

Thank. Thank God for that memory. Realize how God has used it for good. Joseph, in Egypt, did not let his painful memories fester, but he forgave his brothers and told them later that even though they meant it for evil, God had used it for good (Genesis 45).

Thank. Thank God for healing and imagine yourself acting in his healed way.

Application

Some memory problems are caused by the use of chemicals or damage to the brain, and we find it easier to prevent them than to correct them. However, failure to encode material correctly causes other memory problems. Anything one can do to make the material meaningful helps, such as using images or placing the material in categories. People often use mnemonic devices to encode information and give it the cues necessary for retrieval.

Memory Aids

Method of Loci. This uses a series of places already in memory. Take a "mental walk" down your street or through your house and place the material you want to remember in specific places on your "walk." When you need to recall it, take the "walk" again and the material will be there.

Peg system. Hang material to be remembered on a list of "memory pegs" you already have, such as numbers or letters.

Acronyms. Use the first letter of each word in a series to make a new "word." The colors of the spectrum are ROY G. BIV.

Narrative Chaining. When you need to recall a series of words, make them into a story. When you recall the story, you will know the words.

Rhyming. Place the material you need to remember in a rhyme. "I before E except after C, or when sounded as A as in neighbor or weigh."

Code. Organizations know the value of coding phone numbers to letters. If I want to schedule a missionary from OMS International to visit one of my classes, I know to dial (800) CALL OMS.

An Example

As a practical example of using these techniques, let us use them to remember *Psychology from a Christian Perspective*. To place all of psychology in our Christian perspective, look at the entire perspective at the beginning of Chapter 17. Of course, there are many ways to remember all of this material, but at the moment what occurs to me is to use an image and acronyms.

Perhaps you have already noticed that the "framework" of our perspective is the cross, the central symbol of Christianity. The words forming the center and top of our perspective are in boldface type to make them stand out in the form of the cross. At the top we are humans like animals and like God. I can get an image of this with items hanging from each arm of the cross.

The next problem is to remember the areas of psychology which make up the stem of the cross. While working on this chapter, I was riding with a friend when he killed a dog while driving, and he felt very bad. Since the areas of psychology do not have to come in any special order, I remember them all by thinking of what happened on the road, "DOG AAA. I'M SAD, SAD PET." (I have to remember to leave out the "o" in dog, and I think "triple A"--the auto club.)

The stem of the cross becomes (D)efinition, (G)oals, (A)cademic methods, (A)pplied methods, (A)pproaches, (I)ntellect, (M)otivation, (S)tructure, (A)wareness, (D)evelopment, (S)ocial, (A)ssessment, (D)isorders, (P)ersonality, (E)motion, (T)herapy.

Of course, this may not be at all meaningful to you, but it is to me because of the experience I had this week. It may sound crazy to you, but it works for me. You can work out some way of getting it into your long-term memory, remembering that your memory is different from mine.

Chapter 11

Motivation

Motives energize and direct behavior. Some motives arise from the biological condition of our bodies, and we share this biological motivation with animals. Other motives arise from the fact that God made us in his image. For lack of a better term, I call these cognitive motives. Thus motivation appears on both the animal-like and God-like side of our perspective Figure 11.1.

	HUMAN BEINGS IN THE	
CREATED LIKE ANIMALS	**AS WELL AS**	**IMAGE OF GOD LIKE GOD**
Overt Behavior	**DEFINITION**	Mental Processes
Understand Creation	**GOALS**	Make People God-Like
Experimental	**ACADEMIC METHODS**	Descriptive
Behavioral	**APPLIED METHODS**	Cognitive
Behavioristic	**APPROACHES**	Cognitive
Biological	Psychoanalytic	Humanistic
Physiological	**STRUCTURE**	Spiritual
Immaturity	**DEVELOPMENT**	Maturity
Sensation	**AWARENESS**	Perception Consciousness
Learning	**INTELLECT**	Thinking Memory
Biological	**MOTIVATION**	**Cognitive**

Figure 11.1. Motivation from a Christian perspective.

Biological Motivation

To maintain life, people must satisfy their biological needs. They must eat, drink, rest, sleep, maintain body temperature, and, for the species to survive, they must engage in sexual behavior. Animals, likewise, must satisfy the same needs. Psychologists have studied hunger, thirst and sex more than any other biological motives.

Hunger

Animal-like biological mechanisms control hunger to some extent. Damage to neurons in or near one part of the brain results in weight gain, while damage in another results in starvation even with food lying around. The pancreas and the liver also help regulate how much we eat. When blood glucose levels drop, receptors in the liver fire, the brain interprets these as hunger, and people are motivated to eat.

In addition, God-like mental processes influence hunger. Moving up a couple of steps in our perspective, the perception of food can trigger hunger, even when people have just eaten. You may have experienced this when walking past a bakery soon after eating lunch. Moving down a step in our perspective, thinking about our food can erase hunger even when we have not eaten recently. For example, if you get up in the morning and think about eating twice-burned ground plant embryos (toast) covered with solidified secretions of animal mammary glands (butter), and hardened avian embryos (eggs), you may not be very hungry.

Thirst

Animal-like biological mechanisms seem to control thirst entirely. Eating something salty causes water to move out of the cells and people begin to drink. Vomiting or diarrhea takes water from around the cells and individuals begin to drink. Thirst is quite directly tied to loss of water and its effect on the body.

Sex

Animal-like biological mechanisms control human sexual behavior to some extent. The hypothalamus controls, and responds to, the level of the sexual hormones in the body. When we remove sexual hormones in lower animals, sexual behavior stops. In humans, when we remove the sexual hormones, sexual behavior decreases, but it usually continues.

Human sexuality is a part of the image of God in humans. The first chapter of the Bible specifically states that God made us male and female in his Image. It also states that when God considered what he had made, he found it was *very* good. God-like mental processes play a major role in our sexual motivation. For some people the perception of perspiration is erotic, but for others it is offensive. For some people reading pornographic novels is sexually arousing, but for others it is disgusting. Whatever the case, our sexuality involves God-like perceptual and cognitive mental processes.

Some motives are primarily biological, but we must always remember that humans are a unity. Even when hormones and the nervous system basically control our motives, mental processes play a part. Now let us turn to motives on the God-like side of our perspective.

Cognitive Motivation

Although most psychologists agree about biological motivation, they disagree more about cognitive motives. The study of these other motives has come more from personality and social psychology than from experimental psychology.

Self-Actualization

Maslow (1954) proposed a theory of human motivation with needs appearing at different levels. When basic needs are met, growth needs appear. These growth needs are needs for wholeness, perfection, completion, justice, aliveness, richness, simplicity, beauty, goodness, uniqueness, effortlessness, playfulness, truth, and self-sufficiency. Maslow saw these as forming a unity with each being the whole seen from a different angle.

Maslow (1968) noted that these were the attributes assigned to most gods. From our perspective, we agree that these are many of the attributes of God. However, Maslow believed that people had created their gods in their own best image. Christians maintain that God is the original, and that he created us in his image. Of course, "self-actualization" is actualizing our potential to be like God, and a better term might be "God-actualization." Maslow discovered the image of God in humans, but, being an atheist, he has confused the original and the copy.

While God-like self-actualization is the highest level, we must remember that it is last to appear. The lowest level in Maslow's approach was the physiological needs for food, water, sex, and so forth. That is, even though his emphasis was on the God-like, he recognized that humans were also animal-like. We must do the same.

Cognitive Consistency

About mid-century several social psychologists independently began to study what is now called cognitive consistency. People seem to have a need to know, and to have their cognitions (thoughts, beliefs) logically agree with each other. That is, one thought should not be logically the opposite of another.

The consistency theory that generated the most research was Festinger's (1957) theory of cognitive dissonance. He maintained that inconsistent cognitions motivated people to reduce the tension (dissonance) the inconsistency produced. For example, people who want to live a long life, smoke, and believe the Surgeon General's Reports, have dissonance. This dissonance motivates them either to quit smoking or to discount the Surgeon General's Reports.

From our Christian perspective we know God is a consistent, rational God. In his image we want to be the same way. God asks us to reason with him (Isaiah 1) because we, too, are rational beings. Most of the consistency theories have taken the negative approach of avoiding inconsistency, but from our perspective we would put the emphasis on becoming more God-like, of seeking to know and grow.

Before leaving this motive, we must realize that animals also have something of a need to know. They are curious and will learn to respond just for the opportunity to explore. While we are God-like in our cognitive motivation, we are also a bit animal-like.

Love

Psychologists have not said much about love as a motive, but humanistic psychologists have said more than others. May (1969) wrote about four types of love, including agape love. May said that agape love is esteem for the other, concern for the other person's welfare beyond any gain for oneself. He noted that this is the kind of love God shows for humans.

Maslow (1954) studied love in self-actualizing people. He found B-love, love for the being of the other person. It was unneeding love, unselfish love. People welcome this B-love into consciousness, completely enjoy it, and can never get enough of it. B-lovers are not jealous or threatened, and they create their partners--help them on toward self-actualization.

As Christians we say that agape love and B-love are descriptions of the image of God in humans. God is love, and we should love one another because he is love. Jesus said that he had loved us as God had loved him and commanded us to love each other as he loved us (John 15). He pointed out that we are not to love only our friends, but our enemies as well--as God did. As the ultimate example, he gave his life for those who hated him.

Of course, these psychologists also pointed out that humans had animal-like aspects of love too. May (1969) noted there was sex and eros. Maslow (1954) talked about the physiological need for sex and a deficiency love which was a selfish love need. Even in a God-like motive such as love, humans have animal-likenesses.

Implications

Made in God's image, people are spiritual beings. As such, they can sin, and sin often involves motivation. Sins involving physiological motives are often called sins of the flesh while sins involving cognitive motives are often called sins of the spirit.

Sins of the Flesh

People often call outward sins (actually doing something wrong) the sins of the flesh. Although hunger and sex were on the animal-like side of our perspective, people may sin while trying to satisfy them.

Although we do not hear much preaching about it, overeating is a common sin of the flesh in our culture today. We live in a society where food is abundant, and many people are unable to control their appetite for it. Businesses recognize the pervasiveness of this sin. You see advertisements for fattening foods, and right next to them are ads for diet books, exercise videos, and weight-loss centers. Overeating is, quite literally, a sin of the flesh.

Sexual sins are also common in our society. More than three out of four people engage in sexual intercourse before they marry, and more than half in sex outside marriage after they marry. Of course, we have changed the names of these sins to make them sound less evil. Rather than calling them fornication and adultery, we call them premarital and extramarital sex. People used to call homosexual behavior a sin, then they called it a crime, then a mental illness, and beginning in the 1970s, an alternate lifestyle.

Sins of the Spirit

People often call inward sins (not necessarily involving overt activity) the sins of the spirit. The best catalog of these sins is the traditional list of seven deadly sins. Fairlie (1978) notes that they are all demonstrations of love that has gone wrong. Although it is God-like for humans to love, in sin people misplace, weaken, or distort it.

Pride, envy and anger are sins of perverted love. Pride, an overwhelming opinion of one's own qualities, has become acceptable in the individualism and achievement orientation of our culture. Envy assumes that everyone should be able to do, experience, and enjoy everything anyone else can do. Anger arises as a defense of ourselves in the face of a loss of esteem.

Sloth is defective love because people do not give in the proper measure. Sloth is difficult to recognize because it has become so much the norm in our society. Rather than trying to do as much as possible, everyone tries to do an average amount of work. In fact, they may act against those who work too much.

Greed, gluttony, and lust are sins of excessive love. Greed is a sin of the middle class in which people just "have to have" the latest gadget being advertised--while living in abundance, they say they just cannot "get ahead." Gluttony is an inordinate interest in food. Even dieters, who can think about little more than their next meal, may be gluttons. Lust, especially in the sexual sense, appears frequently in our culture in books, magazines, movies, and videos.

Applications

Since many Christians have a problem with overeating (gluttony), they could use many of the techniques developed by psychologists for controlling weight. Of course, no program works for everyone, so some of these methods will work for one person and other methods for another. Of course, before going on a diet-exercise program, check with your doctor to be sure you have no health problem.

First, keep a written record of your what you eat, when you eat, where you eat, how much you exercise, and your thoughts about eating. Most overweight people do not know these basic facts about themselves.

Second, look at your record to identify the stimuli that trigger eating. The sight of food on the table or in a candy dish may trigger eating in one person. The smell does it in another, television in another, and stress in yet another.

Third, change your thoughts and behavior relative to food. Rather than thinking, "I don't have any will power," think, "I can control my eating if I want to." Keep away from stimuli that trigger eating. For example, leave the bowls of food in the kitchen rather than placing them on the table. Stop watching so much television.

Fourth, reward yourself for losing weight--but not by going out to eat! Praise yourself and have friends praise you. Buy yourself a new outfit whenever you lose an additional five pounds.

Finally, exercise. After several weeks of eating less, your body will reduce its metabolic rate, so you will stop losing weight. The best way not only to burn calories, but also increase your metabolic rate, is to exercise.

Chapter 12

Emotion

Closely related to motivation is emotion. In fact, the root of both words is the same, "mot." Emotion is sometimes a motivator. Emotion has been a part of psychology since its beginning. The first system of psychology, structuralism, included "affective states" as one of the three elements of consciousness.

CREATED LIKE ANIMALS	HUMAN BEINGS IN THE AS WELL AS	IMAGE OF GOD LIKE GOD
Overt Behavior	**DEFINITION**	Mental Processes
Understand Creation	**GOALS**	Make People God-Like
Experimental	**ACADEMIC METHODS**	Descriptive
Behavioral	**APPLIED METHODS**	Cognitive
Behavioristic	**APPROACHES**	Cognitive
Biological	Psychoanalytic	Humanistic
Physiological	**STRUCTURE**	Spiritual
Immaturity	**DEVELOPMENT**	Maturity
Sensation	**AWARENESS**	Perception
		Consciousness
Learning	**INTELLECT**	Thinking
		Memory
Biological	**MOTIVATION**	Cognitive
Physiological	**EMOTION**	**Cognitive**

Figure 12.1. Emotion from a Christian perspective.

Although psychologists have yet to agree on a single definition of emotion, their definitions usually include something about conscious experiences or cognitive states on the one hand and bodily states or physiological changes on the other. Thus, emotion appears on both the animal-like and God-like side of our perspective in Figure 12.1.

Although psychologists agree on the components of emotion, they argue about how the parts relate, especially about the order of the cognitive and physiological changes. More than a century ago when American psychologist William James proposed his theory of motivation, he used the example of walking through the woods and meeting a bear. Since this rarely happens today, let us use an example of the same emotion (fear) in a more current setting. Suppose a person steps in front of a moving car. Although psychologists usually agree about what events happen, they do not agree about when they happen.

Common Sense

Taking the common sense approach, many people say that the stimulus (sight of the car) leads to the conscious experience of fear. This fear triggers physiological arousal (heart pounding, adrenaline, etc.) and the response of running. Thus, the order would be the stimulus, followed by the conscious experience of fear, followed by the physiological changes and overt response. This is shown in part (a) of Figure 12.2.

TIME ⟶		⟶	⟶
a. Common Sense	Event	**Conscious** Experience	**Physiological** Changes
b. James- Lange	Event	**Physiological** Changes	**Conscious** Experience
c. Cannon- Bard	Event	Thalamus	**Physiological** Changes **Conscious** Interpretation
d. Schachter- Singer	Event	**Physiological** Changes	**Cognitive** Interpretation
TIME ⟶		⟶	⟶

Figure 12.2. Order of cognitive and physiological events in four theories of emotion.

Note that in the common sense view emotion involves both the God-like mental processes of subjectively experiencing the fear, and the animal-like physiological responses of the pounding heart and running away. This makes intuitive sense--that people run from cars because they are afraid of being hit.

James-Lange

Independently in the mid-1880's William James and Carl Lange proposed an approach to emotion that dominated psychology for many years. Contrasting his approach to the common sense one, James (1884/1968) said, "My thesis on the contrary is that *the bodily changes follow directly the* PERCEPTION *of the exciting fact and that our feeling of the same changes as they occur* IS *the emotion*" (p. 19, Italics in the original).

James agreed that people have both the God-like subjective experiences and the animal-like physiological responses, but he disagreed about the order. When people sense that the car is about to hit them, they run and their hearts start pounding, then they feel the fear. According to him they feel fear because they sense that their hearts are pounding or that they are trembling. When impulses from internal receptors reach the brain, it interprets them as emotional responses. Thus, we feel sorrow because we sense that we are crying and we feel angry because we sense that we are striking.

The James-Lange theory is in part (b) of Figure 12.2. Note that it is much the same as the common sense approach, except that events happen in reverse order. Rather than the fear causing the running, the awareness of the running is the fear.

Cannon-Bard

A little more than forty years later physiologist Walter Cannon (1927) and his student Philip Bard challenged both the common sense and the James-Lange approaches. However, rather than proposing something totally new, they still included both God-like cognitive responses and animal-like physiological responses when people see the car bearing down on them.

Cannon and Bard said that rather than either one occurring first, both occurred at the same time. When the stimuli from the external event reach the thalamus, the thalamus sends neural impulses in two directions at once. It sends impulses to the internal body organs to produce the physiological responses. It also sends impulses to the cerebral cortex where it interprets them as the felt emotion.

As shown in part (c) of Figure 12.2, both animal-like and God-like processes occur, but neither causes the other. They occur simultaneously and independently. The conscious experience occurs at the same time as the bodily reaction. It can occur without the bodily changes, although it is usually intensified by the physiological reactions.

Schachter-Singer

A little less than forty years later Schachter and Singer (1962) proposed a slightly different theory. The James-Lange theory required a different physiological arousal for each emotion, and evidence at the time indicated that all emotions had about the same generalized arousal. If this were true, how could people tell the difference?

Thus, Schachter and Singer (1962) proposed that people interpret this stirred-up state in terms of the immediate situation. When they notice that their heart is pounding, they interpret it as fear if they have just jumped out of the path of a car. However, they interpret it as anger if they are standing with clenched fists, about to strike someone.

Notice that in part (d) of Figure 12.2 this approach still has both the God-like cognitive processes and the animal-like physiological responses. In this case it is the cognition that labels the arousal. In fact, it may not label the arousal as emotion at all. For example, a person may have a pounding heart from jogging, and feel neither fear nor anger.

Other approaches to emotion also emphasize both cognitive and physiological factors. The argument over which comes first is probably a fruitless argument because in real people we cannot separate the cognitive from the physiological. People are unified beings, both animal-like and God-like, and attempts to divide them lose something in the process.

Implications

Although emotions are such an important part of our lives, both secular psychologists and Christians have difficulty with them. In general secular psychologists have difficulty with the positive ones and have tended to ignore them. Positive emotions are difficult to produce and manipulate for study. To study something, scientists want to repeatedly produce, manipulate, and observe it. In addition, although people often see psychologists when frightened or grieving, they rarely do so when peaceful or joyful.

Joy

Christ was characterized as having joy, and having it even when he was facing the cross because he could look beyond it (Hebrews 12). Made in God's image, we are also to have joy, the joy of Christ. He wanted our joy to be full, a joy no one could take from us (John 15-17).

When psychologists have tried to study joy in the laboratory, they have not been able to produce this kind of joy. They have had to study the "joy" that depends on outward circumstances, happiness. Of course, this is a pale reflection of true Christian joy, but psychologists must remember that it exists.

Awe

God's people are told to stand in awe of him (Psalm 4, Psalm 33). However, we find few references in today's psychology to feelings of awe, wonder, or reverence. A naturalistic perspective leaves little room for such feelings, yet people continue to experience them. Maslow (1964) did study these feelings and called them peak experiences. He found them most often as people contemplated nature, God's creation.

Peace

The person controlled by the Spirit has peace (Romans 8). The list of the fruit of the spirit (Galatians 5) includes peace. In the same passage in which Jesus talked about joy, he talked about peace (John 15-17). Psychologists have rarely studied this Christ-like emotion that people have in Christ.

Applications

Psychologists have done much study of the unpleasant emotions because they so often have to work with people experiencing them. In addition, they are easier to produce in the laboratory. However, Christians find these more difficult to discuss, because many Christians believe we should not have them. Christians can learn something about these from psychology.

Sorrow

Although Christians eagerly examine the joy found in Christ, they are often hesitant to discuss the sorrow. They seem to believe it is not God-like to feel sorrow. However, Isaiah called Jesus the "Man of sorrows" (Isaiah 53). When Lazarus died, Jesus "groaned in the spirit, and was troubled" when he saw Mary and the Jews weeping. In fact, "Jesus wept," is the shortest verse in the Bible, but one of the most important (John 11).

Of course, Christian grief is not a hopeless grief because of the promises we have for the future. We must remember that it is real now, and attempts to convince ourselves that it is not here are wrong. Psychologists have recently done much research in death and dying, and their techniques to deal with grief are useful to all.

Anger

While eager to talk about joy, Christians are reluctant to discuss anger. Again, they seem to believe that it is not God-like. That is not the case, because Jesus himself became angry when people misused his father's house (Mark 3). Of course, the Bible tells us not to sin in our anger (Ephesians 5). Anger is one of those emotions that can be sinful at one time and not at another. We must be very careful of our own anger, and less hasty to condemn it in others.

At one time psychologists promoted expressing anger, letting off steam, as being good. However, more recently they have concluded that expressing anger only makes a person more likely to be aggressive again, and probably does little good for the person. Now they say, cool down (count to ten, or a hundred if you need to), try to rethink the problem (because anger depends on your perception), and decide carefully how to express it (before flying off the handle). Note how they bring in the God-like mental processes.

Fear

Unfortunately, translators often translated the Hebrew word meaning "reverence" as the "fear of God." Christians then have the wrong impression when they read that they are to "fear God," because it usually means not to stand "in terror" before him, but to stand "in awe" of him.

Psychologists deal with persons having anxiety or fear (phobias), and in a later chapter we will see how we can reduce such fear by using extinction.

Chapter 13

Personality

Although psychologists have been unable to agree on a common definition of personality, definitions usually involve organizing everything we have discussed up to this point. Personality is the distinctive pattern of behavior and mental processes that characterizes an individual. It includes development, awareness, intellect, motivation and emotion.

	HUMAN BEINGS	
CREATED_____	**IN THE**_____	**IMAGE OF GOD**
LIKE ANIMALS_____	**AS WELL AS**_____	**LIKE GOD**
Overt Behavior	**DEFINITION**	Mental Processes
Understand Creation	**GOALS**	Make People God-Like
Experimental	**ACADEMIC METHODS**	Descriptive
Behavioral	**APPLIED METHODS**	Cognitive
Behavioristic	**APPROACHES**	Cognitive
Biological	Psychoanalytic	Humanistic
Physiological	**STRUCTURE**	Spiritual
Immaturity	**DEVELOPMENT**	Maturity
Sensation	**AWARENESS**	Perception Consciousness
Learning	**INTELLECT**	Thinking Memory
Biological	**MOTIVATION**	Cognitive
Physiological	**EMOTION**	Cognitive
Behavioristic	**PERSONALITY** Psychoanalytic, Trait	**Humanistic**

Figure 13.1. Personality from a Christian perspective.

In previous chapters our approach was one of analysis. We considered one topic at a time, first on the animal-like side of our perspective, then on the God-like side. Now is the time for synthesis. Since human beings are a unity, all these things fit together in a pattern to make up the individuals we know.

As you might expect, personality appears on both the animal-like and the God-like side of our perspective, as shown in Figure 13.1. Also, since personality is the integration of all the aspects we have discussed in an individual, notice that the major theories of personality are primarily the approaches to psychology we considered in Chapter 2.

Behavioristic Approaches

With their emphasis on the animal-like aspects of humans, the strictly behavioristic approaches to personality are the simplest. As the most radical behaviorist, B. F. Skinner rejects the mentalistic concepts on the God-like side of our perspective, so he needs only to account for behavior on the animal-like side.

Skinner's approach is basically that people are more likely to repeat reinforced behavior and less likely to repeat unreinforced behavior. Of course schedules of reinforcement, the sequences of reinforcements and nonreinforcements, have an effect on a person's behavior. Behaviorists have studied these in detail. This approach does account for much behavior, because God created people as he created animals.

As noted earlier, Albert Bandura has extended this basic behavioral approach by adding God-like cognitive variables. That is, reinforcement from the environment does affect behavior, but that does not account for all the behaviors that make up personality. People can also learn by observing others and modeling them. People can get cognitive representations of the behaviors of others. These cognitions then serve as models for their own actions.

This social-cognitive-learning approach, like classical behaviorism, says that our environment influences us. However, it goes a step farther and says that we are not slaves to the environment, but can assess the situation and change our environment. Thus, the behavioristic approach has also come to appreciate the God-like aspects of humans.

Psychoanalytic Approaches

Sigmund Freud (1940/1949) developed psychoanalysis, the first major contemporary theory of personality. Although Freud emphasized the animal-like aspects of humans, he also recognized the God-like ones.

Freud proposed three structures of personality. First was the id, the most basic structure. The id consists of the animal-like instinctual drives that try to get pleasure and avoid pain. Second he proposed the ego, the more God-like rational part of personality. The ego delays satisfactions until conditions are appropriate. Finally was the superego, the most God-like ethical part of personality. The superego was the individual's conscience and a striving toward perfection.

Freud believed that these structures operated at three levels of consciousness. First, the id operated at the unconscious level, where people were completely unaware of what was happening. They could not even bring material in it to awareness. The unconscious was irrational, not like God at all. Second was the preconscious (or subconscious), which was the more God-like memory we have already discussed. It was rational, and people could retrieve material in it whenever they wished. Third was the conscious, which was the God-like consciousness we have talked about.

Although Freud recognized the God-like ego, superego, preconscious, and conscious, for him these were all secondary. The animal-like id was the basic structure of personality and had all the energy. The irrational unconscious was by far the largest, and most important, level of consciousness.

Erik Erikson (1963) continued to use all the structures and levels of consciousness as Freud. However, he maintained that the more God-like ego and consciousness were of greater importance than the id and the unconscious. Many contemporary psychoanalysts, likewise, have put greater emphasis on the God-like aspects of personality.

Trait Approaches

Psychologists taking the trait approach to personality maintain that different traits make up personality. Traits are characteristics that differ from person to person in a relatively permanent and consistent way. One person may be cold, intelligent, cheerful, dominant and suspicious. Another may be warm, dull, depressed, submissive, and friendly.

Gordon Allport (1961) proposed that a few people have a cardinal trait, one which dominates their entire lives. Examples of someone like this are Gandhi, Hitler, or the apostle Paul. Most people have a few central traits which form the building blocks of their personalities. For example, a person may be warm, friendly, intelligent, honest, generous, and sensitive. Finally, we have many secondary traits that come up in specific circumstances. A person may not like spinach, bananas, and bologna.

Trait theories of personality do not fit on either side of our Christian perspective. Some of the traits are more animal-like and some more God-like. Thus, trait theories appear in the center of our perspective in Figure 13.1.

Humanistic Approaches

Humanistic approaches to personality emphasize the God-like aspects of people. The central concept of Carl Rogers' theory of personality is the self, and its definition includes many of the topics discussed on the God-like side of our perspective. The self consists of all the conscious perceptions, thoughts, and values that people believe are characteristic of themselves. This self influences how people see the world and how they behave in it.

The self can develop fully only when people receive unconditional positive regard, God-like love. In addition to this real self, Rogers says we have an ideal self. This is our conception of what we would like to be, usually God-like. The only motive Rogers proposes is the actualizing tendency, the drive to become all we can be, God-like.

Earlier we saw that Abraham Maslow had a similar motive at the top of his list. He saw us as moving toward self-actualization, toward becoming God-like. However, we must remember that Maslow also had the animal-like physiological drives at the base of his list of motives. Even with their emphasis on the God-like, humanists recognized the animal-like.

Implications and Applications

A theory is a way of organizing what we know about a given area, and Christians hold variations on all these theories of personality. Each of these theories emphasize various aspects of personality, and people holding different ones often find themselves in conflict. However, from our Christian perspective, we see that they are complementary rather than in conflict. Where one theory omits something, another theory supplies it.

All of these theories have applications which we will discuss in following chapters. Since theories are means of summarizing many facts, trying to separate Christian implications for each theory and applications of each theory to Christianity is difficult. Therefore, in this chapter we will consider them together.

Religious Behavior

With its emphasis on behavior, the behavioristic approach would say that people do religious behaviors, not to become more God-like, but because such behavior is reinforced. For example, some people may go to church because they find the fellowship with other people rewarding. Others may go to church because that is a good source of contacts for their business.

The behavioristic approach would also say that people do other religious behaviors to avoid punishment. For example, people may read their Bibles and pray daily because they feel guilty when they do not. Their daily devotions then become a matter of avoidance learning. People may give much money to the church to avoid eternal punishment. Their offerings become a "hell insurance policy."

From our Christian perspective, we would say that this does happen some of the time. Paul said that some preach out of envy, rivalry, and selfish ambition (Philippians 1), and we have seen that in the twentieth century. However, Paul goes on to say that others preach sincerely, out of good will. He was happy to see Christ preached whether the motives were false or true. Just because some people's religious behaviors are a result of their animal-like natures does not mean that other people's are not a result of their God-like natures.

Innate Evil

Freud came to the conclusion that the id was evil, and that it could never change. People were born with only the id, and had to learn to live with it for the rest of their lives. They could repress it and suppress it, but they could never get rid of it. The id would always be there in the unconscious, pushing for immediate gratification of its desires.

After years of emphasis on the innate goodness of human beings, or perhaps their neutrality, Maslow (1968) began proposing a psychology of evil. He realized that we cannot get a full view of humanity without considering evil.

Christians call the same thing original sin. Everyone is born with this innate tendency toward evil. Some Christians, like Freud, believe we can do nothing about this tendency until the person dies, or even after. Others believe that God can do something about it even while people are still living. Christians agree that evil is a reality, but they say that Christ conquered evil through his death, and that he can do something about it before a person goes to heaven. Christianity does not leave one with the hopeless pessimism of psychoanalysis.

Religious Traits

Trait theorists would point out that people have religious traits. Most Christians would have a central trait related to religion. This would be one of a half dozen traits that would be a major influence on their lives. Because of their religious trait, they would attend church and give money to it. They would read their Bibles and pray daily. A mature Christian's religious trait would be one of a cluster of traits including the God-likenesses found in humans by Maslow (1968), ones we considered in the chapter on motivation.

Some Christians would have a cardinal trait of religion. Their entire lives would be dominated by their religion. They even center their every conversation on religion. For example, they might not even be able to eat a meal without pointing out that Jesus was the bread of life and that we are to be the salt of the earth. Although we may call them fanatics, they are often the most effective Christians.

Peak Experiences

Humanistic psychologist Abraham Maslow discovered that self-actualizing people had peak experiences. These mystical experiences were often associated with nature, but were high points of the individual's lives.

Conversion experiences are often peak experiences. Of course, they are more than just the naturalistic peak experiences Maslow studied. People describe their personal encounters with God in the same words, but conversion is infinitely more than just a peak experience.

Chapter 14

Assessment

Since psychological assessment basically grew out of the need to measure personality, it also appears on both the animal-like and the God-like side of our perspective in Figure 14.1.

CREATED LIKE ANIMALS	HUMAN BEINGS IN THE AS WELL AS	IMAGE OF GOD LIKE GOD
Overt Behavior	**DEFINITION**	Mental Processes
Understand Creation	**GOALS**	Make People God-Like
Experimental	**ACADEMIC METHODS**	Descriptive
Behavioral	**APPLIED METHODS**	Cognitive
Behavioristic	**APPROACHES**	Cognitive
Biological	Psychoanalytic	Humanistic
Physiological	**STRUCTURE**	Spiritual
Immaturity	**DEVELOPMENT**	Maturity
Sensation	**AWARENESS**	Perception Consciousness
Learning	**INTELLECT**	Thinking Memory
Biological	**MOTIVATION**	Cognitive
Physiological	**EMOTION**	Cognitive
Behavioristic	**PERSONALITY**	Humanistic
	Psychoanalytic, Trait	
Behavior, Unconscious	**ASSESSMENT**	**Self, Intelligence**

Figure 14.1. Assessment from a Christian perspective.

Since each approach to personality emphasized different things, each developed its own measures of personality. In addition, psychologists have developed reliable measures of intelligence, a God-like aspect as shown in Figure 14.1.

Behavioral Observations

Psychologists taking the behavioral approach to personality define personality in terms of behavior. Their major method of measuring personality, then, is to observe behavior. One can observe the behavior of people just as one does that of animals. Psychologists sometimes make these observations casually in unstructured situations, without people even knowing they are being observed. This has the advantage of people acting naturally, not performing for the observer.

More frequently, however, psychologists make observations in more structured settings. They place people in given situations and record reactions. While interviewing someone, psychologists watch posture, facial expression, and gestures as well as listening to the tone of the voice.

While observing, psychologists may use a rating scale, so they can record how much behavior occurred, not only that it happened. However psychologists make the observations, the point here is that they measure human behavior relevant to personality in much the same way they measure the behavior of animals, as shown in Figure 14.1.

Projective Tests

For classical psychoanalysts the most important structure of personality is the id, and it is in the large unconscious part of the mind. As a result, they have tried to develop methods of measuring what is happening in the irrational, animal-like unconscious part of personality, as shown in Figure 14.1.

Projective tests use vague stimuli that people can interpret many different ways. Psychoanalysts ask their patients what they see in the stimuli, usually presented on cards. Since there really is nothing definite on the cards, psychoanalysts assume that whatever the people see comes from their own unconscious.

The Rorschach test is a series of inkblots originally made by placing ink on paper, folding it over and squashing the ink out in all directions. The patient tells the psychoanalyst what the inkblot looks like, much as you look at clouds in the sky and try to see different figures in them. Psychoanalysts then use their theory of personality to interpret what is happening in the patient's unconscious.

The Thematic Apperception Test is a series of pictures of different people, sometimes alone and sometimes with others. Psychoanalysts ask patients to tell a story about what is happening in each picture. Patients tell what led up to the picture, what is happening now, and what will happen. Again the analyst interprets unconscious, animal-like aspects of the story on the basis of psychoanalytic theory.

Self-Reports

Trait theorists and humanistic psychologists are more likely to use some type of paper-and-pencil test to measure psychological traits and the self. Each statement has a limited set of answers. The patients decide whether or not each statement is true about themselves. Since these are verbal, rational approaches to testing, they appear on the God-like side of our perspective in Figure 14.1.

Since Rogers was interested in measuring the self, he often used the Q-sort, a series of statements on cards. He asked clients to sort the cards into seven piles with a given number of statements in each pile. In the first pile the clients placed those statements which they would label as "most like me." They placed the statements "least like me" in the last pile, the statements neither like me or unlike me in the middle pile, and the rest of the statements in the remaining piles. By studying how clients sorted the statements, Rogers knew how they saw themselves.

Some of these tests were much more objective, paper-and-pencil tests, given to large numbers of people, and scored by computers to give scores on different scales or traits. The most widely used test of this type is the Minnesota Multiphasic Personality Inventory, commonly called the MMPI. This test gives scores on ten scales related to mental illness, such as hypochondriasis, depression, psychopathy, paranoia, and schizophrenia.

Objecting to the negative image of such scales, other psychologists developed scales measuring people on more normal personality traits. The California Psychological Inventory scores people on 15 personality traits, such as dominance, sociability, self-control, tolerance, and responsibility. Such traits obviously reflect the God-likenesses of people.

Intelligence Tests

Still a part of measuring people, but developed independently of personality research, are intelligence tests. The French developed the first successful intelligence test shortly after 1900 to pick out children unable to do normal school work.

As with personality, psychologists have not been able to agree on a precise definition of intelligence. However, definitions usually include having the capacity to get and use information. This includes nearly all areas on the God-like side of our perspective. People use perception, memory, reasoning, and cognitive motivation. They have to be conscious of the information, store it, retrieve it, combine it, compare it, and have the motivation to use it. Intelligence testing clearly falls on the God-like side in Figure 14.1.

Since intelligence is a capacity, a potential, psychologists cannot measure it directly. Therefore, to get some idea of what people can get and use, psychologists estimate their potential on the basis of what people have already learned. Of course, we must keep in mind that what is already learned is not a perfect reflection of their capacity.

Alfred Binet developed the first intelligence test to detect children unable to do normal reading, writing, and math in school. A psychologist at Stanford University brought it to the United States and revised it, so it is called the Stanford-Binet test. The basic idea of the test is to compare what a particular child can do with the average child of the same age. A child who can do what the average older child can do is bright, and one who can do only what younger children can do is dull.

A widely used intelligence test for adults, the Wechsler Adult Intelligence Scale, or WAIS, compares how many correct answers an adult can give with those given by other adults of the same age. Psychologists see those who can give more correct answers than average as bright, and those who can give fewer than average answers as dull.

Implications

Psychological testing has taken much criticism in recent years, and that criticism has corrected many problems. For example, at mid-century psychologists often released test scores to almost any "authorized" person inquiring about the persons tested. At the same time psychologists were very reluctant to give results to the people tested. Fortunately, confidentiality is much better now.

However, considering that humans are created in the image of God, we would still raise the issue of deception in testing. Persons being tested know that psychologists are searching for hidden symbols and deep meanings, so they are on guard. They often feel they are being "tricked" because no one tells them what they are revealing. Psychologists are on guard because they know that the clients are. It becomes a game of one trying to outwit the other.

Another issue is that of privacy. We must raise the issue of whether or not an employer or a teacher has a right to ask about a person's fears, hatreds, and home life. A person also has a right not to be required to even think about certain topics. For example, the sexually-oriented topics found on some personality tests may lead an individual into temptation.

From our Christian perspective, I believe we should be open and honest in our assessment. Some have repeatedly proposed this, but large numbers of psychologists have never adopted it. Kelly (1955) proposed what many now call the credulous attitude. If you do not know what is wrong with patients, ask them. That is, have a straightforward talk with them in an interview situation. This does not mean that their accounts of events will necessarily agree with the way others saw events. Nevertheless, one should respect what patients say and examine various accounts.

Application

As Christians, we must beware of how we use tests. We live in a society that operates on a credentials system where credentials become more important than people and what they can do. Credentials include educational records, mental health records, test scores, and Boy Scout merit badges. These have become the primary basis for judgment in our society, and they are becoming increasingly important in the church.

To get into college people need the right high school credentials and test scores (diploma and high enough ACT or SAT). To get into seminary people need the right college credentials and test scores (degree and satisfactory MMPI score in many). Thus our church leaders are now chosen by a series of admissions committees based on their credentials. These credentials include tests developed to place the mentally retarded in classes and classify the mentally ill. This is quite different from the list of characteristics Paul gave for church leaders (1 Timothy 3). He mentioned hardworking, thoughtful, orderly, hospitable, gentle, and kind, with well-behaved children and non-gossiping wives.

We must remember that the best predictor of future behavior is past behavior in the same situation. Hilgard, Atkinson, and Atkinson (1975) noted the "annoying tendency" of all kinds of personality tests to yield validity coefficients of about +.30. After many years of effort, psychologists have been unable to raise this validity. If fact, the best predictor of whether or not people will be readmitted to a mental hospital is not a psychological test, but the thickness of their files. The more often and longer they have been in the hospital, the more likely they are to return.

The correlation between SAT scores and first-year grade-point averages in college is +.38 for the verbal and +.35 for the mathematical portions (Linn, 1982). The correlation between SAT scores and GRE scores (Graduate Record Examination) taken four years later is +.86 for the verbal and +.86 for the mathematical portions (Angoff, 1988). Again, past behavior is the best predictor of future behavior. How people score on a test is a better predictor of how they will score on another test than of how well they will do in school.

Finally, test scores and grades in college have very little to do with later occupational success (McClelland, 1973). This means that we should look at what people are doing now to tell what they will do in the future. Test scores tell us something when we have no other data, but let us not rely on them when we have other data.

Chapter 15

Disorders

CREATED LIKE ANIMALS	HUMAN BEINGS IN THE AS WELL AS	IMAGE OF GOD LIKE GOD
Overt Behavior	DEFINITION	Mental Processes
Understand Creation	GOALS	Make People God-Like
Experimental	ACADEMIC METHODS	Descriptive
Behavioral	APPLIED METHODS	Cognitive
Behavioristic	APPROACHES	Cognitive
Biological	Psychoanalytic	Humanistic
Physiological	STRUCTURE	Spiritual
Immaturity	DEVELOPMENT	Maturity
Sensation	AWARENESS	Perception Consciousness
Learning	INTELLECT	Thinking Memory
Biological	MOTIVATION	Cognitive
Physiological	EMOTION	Cognitive
Behavioristic	PERSONALITY	Humanistic
	Psychoanalytic, Trait	
Behavior, Unconscious	ASSESSMENT	Self, Intelligence
Maladjustment	**DISORDERS**	**Adjustment**

Figure 15.1. Disorders from a Christian perspective.

Psychologists deal with more than personality and its assessment. Many of them diagnose and treat disorders of the personality. Although psychologists work with many different disorders, from our perspective we can generally say that in our disorders (maladjustment) we become less like God and in our adjustment we become more like him. This means that this topic also appears on both the animal-like and the God-like sides in Figure 15.1. Maladjustment is not necessarily more animal-like, but since we have no other dimension on our graph, I placed it there.

Maladjustment

Psychologists usually classify abnormal behavior into about a dozen major categories, those specified by the American Psychiatric Association. As we consider these disorders one at a time, we will see that they involve all the areas of psychology we have discussed in our Christian perspective. Let us now consider these in the order they would appear in our perspective, beginning with the structure of humans (Figure 15.2).

	HUMAN BEINGS	
CREATED LIKE ANIMALS	**IN THE**	**IMAGE OF GOD LIKE GOD**
Physiological	**STRUCTURE**	Spiritual
	(Organic Mental Disorders)	(Personality Disorders)
Immaturity	**DEVELOPMENT**	Maturity
	(Disorders First Evident in Infancy, Childhood or Adolescence)	
Sensation	**AWARENESS**	Perception
	(Somatoform Disorders)	(Paranoid Disorders)
		Consciousness
		(Substance Use Disorders)
Learning	**INTELLECT**	Thinking
		(Schizophrenic Disorders)
		Memory
		(Dissociative Disorders)
Biological	**MOTIVATION**	Cognitive
	(Sexual Disorders)	
Physiological	**EMOTION**	Cognitive
	(Anxiety Disorders, Mood Disorders)	

Figure 15.2. Maladjustment from a Christian perspective.

Organic Mental Disorders

Mental health professionals classify people as having organic mental disorders when known functioning of the brain is impaired. Symptoms vary widely, but they are caused by strokes, too little blood getting to the brain, infection, tumors, and so forth. These disorders in structure are on the animal-like side of our perspective.

Personality Disorders

People with a narcissistic personality have an overblown sense of self-importance. They are insensitive to the needs of others but are preoccupied with fantasies of their own success, always needing admiration and attention. Antisocial personalities have little sense of responsibility or morality. They care little about others and have little guilt, even when they cause others much suffering. With this concern for self and lack of a conscience, personality disorders are on the God-like side of our perspective at the level of the structure of persons.

Disorders First Evident in Infancy, Childhood or Adolescence

These disorders obviously are at the level of development in our Christian perspective (Figure 15.2). They include many things familiar to college students. While in elementary school, most students knew someone who was mentally retarded or hyperactive. In high school most students know someone who had an eating disorder such as anorexia nervosa or bulimia.

Somatoform Disorders

The symptoms of the somatoform disorders appear to be physical, but have no known physiological cause. Hypochondriacs feel discomfort in some part of their body and immediately interpret it as some terrible illness. People with conversion disorders suddenly lose a sensory function or become paralyzed. For example, individuals may lose the ability to feel any sensations from a band around their heads. Since these disorders often involve the senses, we can place them on the animal-like side of our perspective at the level of awareness (Figure 15.2).

Paranoid Disorders

Paranoid individuals have a system of delusions in which they usually believe people are persecuting or exploiting them, at least they perceive themselves in this way. They feel mistreated, taken advantage of, spied on, stolen from, and so forth. They usually blame other people for their problems. Whenever anyone questions their delusions, paranoids become suspicious of the questioner, too. When paranoids see two people talking and laughing in the distance, they conclude that the two people are talking about them. This is basically a disorder of perception on the God-like side of our perspective at the level of awareness (Figure 15.2).

Substance Use Disorders

We have already discussed the use of drugs to alter states of consciousness. Some of these chemicals are physiologically addicting, so that the nervous system will not function normally without them. People may become psychologically dependent on other drugs, even if they are not physiologically addicting. These disorders are on the God-like side of our perspective at the level of consciousness (Figure 15.2).

Schizophrenic Disorders

Schizophrenics are characterized by a loss of contact with reality and disturbances in thought. They tend to withdraw from others and have delusions. Their speech may become rambling and disjointed. Some of them make up new words or use common words in a unique way. Others become so bad that there seems to be no relationship between their words at all, words just emerge in a random order. Although schizophrenics also show disturbances in perception and emotion as well, we can place them at the level of intellect in our Christian perspective (Figure 15.2).

Dissociative Disorders

As the name suggests, these disorders involve a dissociation, or splitting of parts of the personality that are normally together. They also involve a lack of memory for some parts of the personality. People with multiple personalities may alternate between several distinct, integrated, well-developed personalities. Some of the personalities may be totally unaware of the others. People with amnesia are unable to remember their names, do not know where they live, and do not recognize close friends or relatives. Since dissociative disorders involve memory, we can place them at that level on the God-like side of our perspective (Figure 15.2).

Sexual Disorders

Some people have problems knowing their sexual identity. Others become sexually aroused by unusual stimuli, such as animals or inanimate objects. They cannot become sexually aroused by an individual of the opposite sex alone, but need their own unique stimulus for arousal. Still others become sexually aroused by children, pain, or humiliation. Some people have problems becoming sexually aroused or having sexual orgasms. Since these involve sexual motivation, they are in our perspective at the level of motivation (Figure 15.2).

Anxiety Disorders

As shown by the label, anxiety is the major symptom in these disorders. Some people have mild anxiety all the time, while others have severe attacks of it at periodic intervals. Still others have intense fears only in certain situations or if they do not carry out particular activities. Some people carry out elaborate rituals to prevent anxiety. Since the major symptom is an emotion, these disorders can be placed at that level in our perspective (Figure 15.2).

Mood Disorders

Mood disorders involve great changes in feeling. Some people are greatly depressed. Others are highly elated. Still others alternate between periods of depression and elation. Since these disorders involve the emotions, they are at that level in our perspective (Figure 15.2).

The American Psychiatric Association has another major category of abnormal behaviors that are not attributable to mental disorders. These include grief over the death of a loved one, problems at work or school, and problems among family members. These problems seem to be social problems which are in our perspective at the level of social psychology, the last chapter in the book.

Implications

Most psychologists agree on the characteristics of abnormal behavior or maladjustment. Behavior which is atypical, maladaptive, socially unacceptable, and brings personal distress is abnormal. For example, people with anxiety disorders are different from others, their anxiety interferes with a normal life, other people do not like their fears, and they are unhappy.

Does this mean that people who are typical, adapted, socially accepted, and happy are adjusted? If so, the Nazi prison camp guard who succeeded at allowing no escapes and was happy in his work was adjusted. Psychologists have struggled with what it means to be adjusted, and definitions vary widely.

From our Christian perspective we would say that to be adjusted means to be like God. We have something outside humanity to define mental health. We have God himself. While God-likeness may seem unattainable, "Christ-likeness" seems less so. When thinking of Christ, people are likely to think of his human attributes as well as his divine ones. Then being like him seems feasible. We considered some of the attributes of God in Chapter 11, and all of these are attainable for us.

While only Christ reveals our full potential, for models we may look at others who are God-like and whose lives reveal something of our potential. The apostle Paul unashamedly told others to pattern their lives after his (Philippians 3-4). We can look at the heroes of the faith (Hebrews 11), both of the past and of the present. Of course, caution is in order when doing this. Whenever looking at the God-like characteristics of anyone other than Christ himself, we must be careful that we are looking at the "in Christ" characteristics of that individual.

Application

Some Christians seem to believe that all mental illness is the result of demon possession. Knowing the mental disorders and some of their causes can help us make a distinction between such disorders and demon possession. In addition, the Bible itself makes the distinction.

Demon possession was relatively rare in the Old Testament, although the Bible strongly suggests it in some passages. Under the influence of a tormenting spirit, Saul was very jealous and violent, attempting to kill David and his own son, Jonathan. However, not all odd behavior was attributed to evil spirits. Only two chapters later, David pretended to be crazy because he was afraid of an enemy king (1 Samuel 19-21). David drooled into his beard and scratched on doors until the king concluded that David must be mad. There is no indication that he pretended to be demon possessed, only that he pretended to be mad.

Demon possession was common in the New Testament. It resulted in violence, the inability to speak, blindness, falling into fire or water, great strength, uncontrolled movements, foaming at the mouth, grinding of the teeth, and rigidity. Of course, many of these "symptoms" are the same as those of the mentally ill and epileptic of today. Yet Jesus distinguished between illness and demon possession even when the symptoms were the same. Once when two blind men came to him, he healed them by touching their eyes. Later people brought a man who was blind and dumb to Jesus. Jesus healed him by casting out a demon (Matthew 9, 12). In one case blindness was caused by demon possession, in another it was not.

Demon possession can cause behavior that is not God-like, but it is not the only cause of such behavior. Although most Christians have not done so, they must clearly state the differences between demon possession and other disorders. Sall (1976) made a clinical distinction between demon possession and other disorders. He noted that demons are anti-Christ, while psychotics often fantasize religious experience. Demons are separate beings, while psychotic experiences are the result of withdrawal from reality. Demons are rational beings, while psychotics are irrational. Demons are object related, while psychotics suffer from a loss of object reality.

Chapter 16

Therapy

CREATED LIKE ANIMALS	HUMAN BEINGS IN THE AS WELL AS	IMAGE OF GOD LIKE GOD
Overt Behavior	DEFINITION	Mental Processes
Understand Creation	GOALS	Make People God-Like
Experimental	ACADEMIC METHODS	Descriptive
Behavioral	APPLIED METHODS	Cognitive
Behavioristic	APPROACHES	Cognitive
Biological	Psychoanalytic	Humanistic
Physiological	STRUCTURE	Spiritual
Immaturity	DEVELOPMENT	Maturity
Sensation	AWARENESS	Perception Consciousness
Learning	INTELLECT	Thinking Memory
Biological	MOTIVATION	Cognitive
Physiological	EMOTION	Cognitive
Behavioristic	PERSONALITY	Humanistic
	Psychoanalytic, Trait	
Behavior, Unconscious	ASSESSMENT	Self, Intelligence
Maladjustment	DISORDERS	Adjustment
Behavioral	THERAPY	**Humanistic**
Biological	Psychoanalytic	**Cognitive**

Figure 16.1. Therapy from a Christian perspective.

gists' conceptions of personality and its assessment influence
.ain abnormality and give therapy. Therapy, then, appears on
b.   imal-like and the God-like sides of our perspective in Figure
16.1.   .hough trait theorists have developed extensive theories of
persona..ty, they have not developed distinct therapies, so they do not
appear in the figure. Although their theories of personality have not
become as popular as the ones discussed in Chapter 13, cognitive theorists
have developed widely used therapies, so they do appear in Figure 16.1.

Behavioristic Therapies

According to the behavioristic approach to personality, people learn
abnormal behaviors just as they learn normal ones. Children frightened
when a dog is present learn to fear dogs through classical conditioning.
The boy who gets his way by hitting people becomes the school bully
through instrumental conditioning. The woman who receives much
sympathy for weeping finds that reinforcing and becomes depressed. Thus,
if the problem is that people have learned the wrong responses, then
therapy becomes a matter of their learning the right responses.

Classical Conditioning Therapies

Behaviorists have developed several therapies using classical
conditioning. Probably the most widely used is systematic desensitization.
It gradually extinguishes the fear people experience in a phobic or anxiety
disorder. Slowly and systematically psychologists confront patients with
fear-producing stimuli until the patients are able to relax in the presence
of something that formerly caused great fear. This is like an animal
learning not to fear a box in which the experimenter had shocked it.

Operant Conditioning Therapies

Behaviorists have developed therapies using operant conditioning, as
well. Some methods involve extinction, similar to the situation described
above. Others involve giving positive reinforcement for desired behavior.
For example, if schizophrenics refuse to talk, psychologists may first give
them candy for making a sound, any sound. Later psychologists reinforce
them for saying a single word, then for a phrase, and finally for a sentence.
They gradually learn to talk using reinforcement, much as you would train
a rat to press a bar. The behavioral therapies are on the animal-like side
of our perspective, as shown in Figure 16.1.

Biological Therapies

Another approach to therapy widely used, not by psychologists, but by people with medical degrees, is the biological approach. This approach assumes that something is wrong with a person's anatomy or physiology, so this therapy goes on the animal-like side of our perspective in Figure 16.1.

Chemotherapy

Some people believe that abnormal behavior is caused by the wrong concentration of neurotransmitters in the synapses. They attempt to remedy this by giving the person drugs. If the person feels anxiety, they give anti-anxiety drugs, tranquilizers. If the patient is depressed, they give anti-depressants. If the person has delusions and hallucinations, they give anti-psychotic drugs.

Psychosurgery

Other people believe that abnormal behavior is caused by problems within the neurons. They attempt to remedy this by using brain surgery. This was very popular at mid-century, when thousands of patients had their frontal lobes severed from the hypothalamus to reduce violence and emotionality.

Electroconvulsive Therapy

Still others treat abnormal behavior by passing electrical currents through the patients' brains to produce convulsions and unconsciousness. This also was very popular at mid-century, but psychiatrists now basically use it for depressed patients who do not respond to drug therapy. All of these change our animal-like anatomy or physiology.

Psychoanalytic Therapies

According to the psychoanalytic approach to personality, unconscious conflicts cause abnormal behavior. During childhood the superego and ego repress conflicts into the unconscious. During stressful times in adulthood these conflicts express themselves in abnormal symptoms. For example, people may have obsessions or compulsions to keep from thinking about hurting a parent who mistreated them as children. To relieve this disorder, psychoanalysts believe patients must become aware of the source of their conflict and deal with it. Because this approach puts the problem in the un-Godlike unconscious, but insists on it being brought to consciousness, I have placed this therapy in the middle of Figure 16.1.

Free Association

While patients are lying relaxed on a couch, their egos are less on guard about what gets from the unconscious to the conscious. Psychoanalysts urge patients to relax and say everything that comes into consciousness, regardless of whether or not it makes sense or is socially acceptable. Analysts then interpret the meaning of these free associations in terms of psychoanalytic theory.

Dream Analysis

While asleep, the ego is even less on guard. Therefore, analysts ask patients to tell everything they remember about their dreams. Of course, dreams often seem ridiculous to us, but analysts believe they can find hidden meanings of things trying to slip into consciousness. They interpret the dreams to patients, again in terms of psychoanalytic theory.

Humanistic Therapies

According to the humanistic approach to personality, abnormal behavior results from people not realizing their full potential. For example, people may have low self-esteem and experience anxiety in the presence of important people because the patients have never been able to develop themselves. Humanistic therapists try to create conditions in which these unsure persons will develop their God-like potentials, as shown in Figure 16.1.

Carl Rogers' (1959) person-centered therapy is the most widely used humanistic therapy. He first called it non-directive, because he emphasized the method. Later he called it client-centered, because the client essentially controlled what happened. Recently he started calling it person-centered, because he wanted the emphasis more clearly on the human values he emphasized.

Rogers believed that people had, within themselves, the resources for changing their self-concepts. However, those resources needed a particular climate if they were to be effective. First, they needed genuineness on the part of the therapist, not a professional facade where the therapist tried to be an objective observer. Second, they needed empathic understanding in which the therapist used active listening to try to see the world from the perspective of the client. Finally, the client needed to receive unconditional positive regard from the therapist. This genuineness and God-like love places person-centered therapy on the God-like side of our perspective in Figure 16.1.

Cognitive Therapy

According to the cognitive approach to personality, abnormal behavior is a result of faulty ways of thinking about the world. Depressed individuals may both believe that they have no control over what happens in their lives and blame themselves for everything that goes wrong. Unlike psychoanalysis, which tries to change the irrational unconscious, cognitive therapy tries to make conscious thinking more rational. Thus, cognitive therapy clearly falls on the God-like side of our Christian perspective in Figure 16.1.

Aaron Beck (1976) is the chief proponent of cognitive therapy for depression. An example will illustrate what one might do in cognitive therapy. Suppose a client did not receive an invitation to a party. He thinks that everyone will notice he is not at the party, decide he is not part of the "in" crowd, and never invite him to a party again. Of course, he is depressed. The therapist helps him see that some people will not even notice he is absent because many people come and go over the course of an evening. Those who do notice may think that he had something else to do, so that he could not come. Furthermore, most people do not make up guest lists for their own parties while at someone else's party.

These are only the most distinct of therapies psychologists use. Furthermore, people may use combinations of these. Cognitive behavior therapy, combining both animal-like and God-like aspects of humans, is very popular right now. In addition, psychologists often have physicians prescribe drugs for their patients to take while they are in some type of therapy with the psychologist.

Implications

Notice in Figure 16.1 that here, in the next to the last chapter of the book, we have returned to where we were in the second chapter. The five major approaches to psychology each have their own approach to therapy. As we noted in Chapter 2, each approach makes particular assumptions about the nature of human beings. Figure 16.2 lists their position on some of the assumptions which have implications for therapy.

	Free-Determined	Good-Evil	Rational-Irrational	Conscious-Unconscious
Behavioral	Determined	Neither	Neither	Neither
Biological	Determined	Neither	Neither	Neither
Psychoanalytic	Determined	Evil	Irrational	Unconscious
Humanistic	Free	Good	Rational	Conscious
Cognitive	Free	Neither	Rational	Conscious
Christian	Both	Both	Both	Both

Figure 16.2. A comparison of the major assumptions about human beings made by the major approaches to therapy.

All of these approaches fit into our Christian perspective because the historic Christian position on these issues is that humans are both, as seen in Figure 16.2. Humans are bound by sin, but free in Christ; created good in God's image, but fallen into evil sin; able to reason with God, but often making irrational choices; and conscious of themselves, but sometimes deceiving even themselves.

In addition, from our Christian perspective, we would add that if the problem is sin, what the patient needs is forgiveness. This comes through confession, repentance, and faith. If the problem is demonic possession, what the patient needs is to have the demon cast out. Chemicals and therapy will not cure spiritual problems.

Application

The therapies have obvious application in the church. Most pastors receive training in counseling. Some churches have Ministers of Counseling who spend all their time giving therapy to parishioners. The church was quick to grasp this use of psychology, but questions have arisen relative to the effectiveness of therapy.

At mid-century Hans Eysenck (1952) published a study evaluating the results of psychotherapy. He found that about two-thirds of the people who received psychotherapy improved, but so did about two-thirds of those who received no therapy. Although psychologists questioned his research, it was nearly 30 years before they showed conclusive evidence that therapy helped.

Using meta-analysis to combine the results of 475 studies, Smith, Glass, and Miller (1980) found that about 80% of those who received therapy were better off than the average person who received no therapy. Although this is not as good as it sounds at first (because 50% of those who receive no therapy are better off than the average), it does mean that therapy, in general, does help.

They also asked the question of whether or not one therapy was better than another. No therapy was consistently better than any other. In addition, it made no difference whether it was group or individual therapy, whether it was short or long, and whether the therapist was inexperienced or experienced. What this all says is that therapy helps most people some, but it is no cure-all.

Therapy is certainly a valuable tool Christians can use in the church, but they must not think that it solves the problem of sin. Only forgiveness from God himself is effective for that.

Chapter 17

Social Psychology

CREATED LIKE ANIMALS	HUMAN BEINGS IN THE AS WELL AS	IMAGE OF GOD LIKE GOD
Overt Behavior	**DEFINITION**	Mental Processes
Understand Creation	**GOALS**	Make People God-Like
Experimental	**ACADEMIC METHODS**	Descriptive
Behavioral	**APPLIED METHODS**	Cognitive
Behavioristic	**APPROACHES**	Cognitive
Biological	Psychoanalytic	Humanistic
Physiological	**STRUCTURE**	Spiritual
Immaturity	**DEVELOPMENT**	Maturity
Sensation	**AWARENESS**	Perception Consciousness
Learning	**INTELLECT**	Thinking Memory
Biological	**MOTIVATION**	Cognitive
Physiological	**EMOTION**	Cognitive
Behavioristic	**PERSONALITY** Psychoanalytic, Trait	Humanistic
Behavior, Unconscious	**ASSESSMENT**	Self, Intelligence
Maladjustment	**DISORDERS**	Adjustment
Behavioral	**THERAPY**	Humanistic
Biological	Psychoanalytic	Cognitive
Like God	**SOCIAL**	**Like Animals**

Figure 17.1. Social Psychology from a Christian perspective.

In this last chapter, we arrive at the other end of the spectrum of psychology. We began in the part of psychology closely related to biology, moved through the core of psychology, and are now at the part of psychology closely related to sociology. Social psychology is the study of individuals in society, and it is on both the animal-like and the God-like sides of our perspective in Figure 17.1.

Like Animals

Humans, like animals, live together in pairs and/or in societies. Let us begin our social psychology by considering some parallels between humans and animals.

Bonding

Ethologists, biologists studying animal behavior, found that some animals form pair-bonds, often going through an elaborate ritual to form the bond. Desmond Morris (1971) reviewed these courtship behaviors in animals and specified a series of twelve steps he saw humans taking to form similar bonds. Sex researchers William Masters and Virginia Johnson (1975) echoed this when they named their book *The Pleasure-Bond*. Don Joy (1985) explored the implications of this bonding process from a Christian point of view.

Animal Societies

Some animal societies have obvious status hierarchies. One can watch a flock of chickens on any farm and see their pecking-order. That is, if there are ten chickens, the top chicken can peck any of the nine below. The second from the top can peck any of the eight below, but not the one above. The poor bottom chicken can peck no one. This is so obviously parallel to human society that we even use the term pecking-order to refer to humans.

The hierarchy among primates is more complex. The status of a male baboon depends not only on his personal attributes, but also on his relationship with other males. Among monkeys when a high-ranking mother is present, her young feed in advance of many adult males. This fact complicates the hierarchy.

Aggression

During the mid-1960s several popular books appeared relating aggression in animals to aggression in humans. These primarily con-centrated on linking aggression to territory, dominance hierarchies, and sexual behavior. Konrad Lorenz (1963/1966) argued that because of aggression animals are spread out over adequate territory, the best mother and father reproduce, and an organized community protects the offspring. Although aggression is innate, rituals usually inhibit the expression of aggression, so full-blown aggressive behavior seldom occurs. Lorenz believed humans had mechanisms similar to those in animals.

Obedience

Stanley Milgram (1963) found that subjects in experiments would obediently flip switches, thinking they were giving painful and very dangerous electrical shocks to other people. They did this when told to do so by someone in authority, even when the people they were "shocking" were screaming in pain. Although this surprised many people, we must remember that society had rewarded these subjects for obedience and punished them for disobedience for decades. People, like animals, repeat reinforced behaviors.

Conformity

Solomon Asch (1955) found that subjects would conform to what the rest of the group said, even when asked to make simple perceptual judgments. About one-third of the time people said what the rest of the group said, even though it was wrong. Again we must remember that society has rewarded these people for conforming year after year. People, like animals, repeat reinforced behavior.

Of course, God-like, cognitive factors play a role in social behavior, as in all other behavior. The point here is that animal-like factors play a role as well.

Like God

Several topics in social psychology related to the God-likeness of humans appear rather regularly.

Attributes

A central concept in social psychology is attitudes. Although attitudes predispose us to act in social situations, they are basically cognitive and on the God-like side of our Christian perspective. Sometimes attitudes change our actions, and sometimes our actions change our attitudes. Since we are unified beings, the influence is both ways.

Attributions

Attributions are the explanations a person gives for someone's behavior or beliefs. They may attribute behavior to internal factors or to external factors. When people make such attributions, they are better able to understand or explain events. These attributions are on the God-like side of our perspective because they are social cognitions.

Altruism

When people help others, not expecting personal gain from their action, we call it altruism, or helping behavior. Social psychologists have studied the conditions under which people are more or less likely to get involved in helping others in need. Increasing the clarity of the emergency, and making it obvious that the person has some responsibility for helping increases the likelihood that someone will get involved. People alone are more likely to help than people in a crowd.

Implications

In this last chapter of the book, we return to where we began (Genesis 1) to complete our Christian perspective. God himself is a social being in that he is a trinity of persons, three in one. Before he created humans, he was a social being communing with himself. As scripture notes, God said, "Let *us* make man in *our* image."

Five times in the first chapter of Genesis God looked at some new aspect of his creation and saw that it was good. After creating humanity, he noted that it was *very* good. The first thing in all of creation that was not good was that Adam was alone. God brought birds and animals to Adam who named them, but not one of them was adequate to satisfy his loneliness. Only another person, also made in God's image, could satisfy that loneliness. Although psychologists often discuss pair-bonding in the context of animal societies, such an approach cannot fully explain marriage and the church.

Marriage

Christian marriage is more than pair-bonding. God created us "male and female" in his image (Genesis 1). Our very masculinity and femininity is part of the image of God in us. Following chapters in Genesis point out that a man and woman leave their parents and join so that the two become one flesh.   The two-becoming-one in the marriage relationship is a reflection of the three-in-one of the Trinity.   The biblical reason for limiting sexual intercourse (the one-flesh relationship) to marriage is this trinitarian image of God in humans, the very nature of humans themselves.

The Church

The Bible refers to the church, the subgroup of overall society in which Christians find themselves, as part of the image of God. It refers to the church as the body of Christ, with different members playing various roles, forming a complex organism. Just as the different parts of the human body have different functions and all are needed and useful, so it is with members of the church, the body of Christ. The most important thing about these different roles is that they all make up the one body of Christ. Whenever the Bible discusses these different roles, the emphasis is on unity, not division.

Applications

The topics of social psychology are intimately related to Christianity. Too often in our culture we try to make Christianity an individual religion when God made a covenant with his people, more than just a covenant with individual persons.

Animal-like

Although we may be shocked by Milgram's experiments, in which people obediently followed directions though they believed they were hurting others, we must not come to the conclusion that obedience is always bad. In fact, most of the time it is good. Children are instructed to obey their parents (Ephesians 6), and, more generally, we are told to obey those in authority over us (Romans 13). The obedience demonstrated by social psychologists is good, unless the person in authority tells us to do something wrong. We must make decisions about whether or not to obey using our God-like cognitive ability relative to our conscience.

Likewise, conformity is usually good. Knowing we have the tendency to conform, we can use our God-like freedom of choice to pick the group to which we will conform. We can choose as our closest friends people who are trying to model their lives on the image of God as well. Conformity in this situation will not always be correct, but it will be a large part of the time.

God-like

Although attitudes involve our God-like cognitive processes, they can be wrong. We can have attitudes of prejudice that will lead to discrimination against other groups. Even the Apostle Paul, as a mature Christian, had prejudiced attitudes. He wrote to Titus that one of the Cretans had said that all Cretans were liars, evil beasts, and lazy gluttons (Titus 1). Paul went on to say that the statement was true. We must be careful that our attitudes are correct, and not incorrectly judgmental.

As Christians, we are to help others. However, even knowing that and being reminded of it, we may become bystanders when others are in need of help. Darley and Batson (1973) wanted to find out if thinking about altruism would make people more likely to help. Unfortunately, it made little difference. They found that people in a hurry to give a talk about the Good Samaritan literally stepped over someone in need of help. We must become aware of our tendency to overlook others' needs, especially when we are in a hurry.

Appendix

Statistics

Statistics is the branch of mathematics used to describe and interpret the data gathered in research. Logically we should have discussed statistics in Chapter 2, following the academic methods. However, since the very word itself often brings to mind "impossible," complex formulas, most authors place statistics in an appendix. Used to analyze data from both experimental and descriptive research, statistics appears on both the animal-like and God-like sides of our perspective in Figure 18.1.

	HUMAN BEINGS	
CREATED_____	IN THE_____	IMAGE OF GOD
LIKE ANIMALS_____	AS WELL AS_____	LIKE GOD
Overt Behavior	**DEFINITION**	Mental Processes
Understand Creation	**GOALS**	Make People God-Like
Experimental	**ACADEMIC METHODS**	Descriptive
Inferential	**STATISTICS**	**Descriptive**

Figure 18.1. Statistics from a Christian perspective.

Inferential Statistics

As mentioned in Chapter 2, Daniel suggested an experiment to the official caring for him and his friends while they were being educated to serve in the palace. Of course, scientists have refined the experimental method since that time, but let us imagine how that official might have carried out the experiment and used inferential statistics (if they had existed back then).

From what the Bible says, there were two groups. The official fed one group royal food and wine for ten days. He fed the other group vegetables and water for the same ten days. Other than the difference in diet, he treated both groups the same. At the end of the ten days, he rated each person in both groups (perhaps on a scale of 1 to 10) as to how "healthy" and how "well nourished" each looked.

On the day he rated them some "chance" factors might have influenced the ratings. For example, when the official was rating one person, the wind might have blown just right so his hair had a "healthy wind-blown look" at that moment. Another person might have had the flu so that he looked "pale and malnourished" that day. The official might have come to the wrong conclusion because of these chance factors.

Experimenters today would use inferential statistics to decide whether the difference between the groups on the two different diets was a "real" difference, or was due to chance. The most commonly used inferential statistics today are the t-test and analysis of variance. However, because the data gathered by the official was in the form of a rating scale, he would have had to use some other test, such as a Mann-Whitney U test.

The experimental method with its controls, followed by the use of inferential statistics, allows us to draw cause-effect conclusions. Psychologists investigating animal-like aspects of people can be quite sure about one thing causing another, such as a diet of vegetables and water resulting in better health than a diet of rich foods and alcohol.

Descriptive Statistics

As noted in Chapter 2, strict experimental control is often not possible, especially when investigating God-like aspects. Therefore, scientists use the descriptive methods followed by descriptive statistics to summarize the data. Of course, scientists can use descriptive statistics on animal-like aspects as well.

Central Tendency

Measures of central tendency are averages, and you already know some of them. Statisticians use these to summarize large amounts of data into a single number or two. Psychologists may count the number of correct answers on a test for many people. They then calculate a single number that is about the "center" of all the numbers or the average.

We can find data in the Bible on which we can calculate such averages. Where would we find such data but in the book of Numbers? While they were in the desert after leaving Egypt, God told Moses to take a census. On one particular day he listed the names of all the men over twenty years old one by one, and there were more than half a million names.

To begin to organize this mass of data, they grouped everyone according to ancestry. There were 46,500 descendants of Reuben, 59,300 descendants of Simeon, 45,650 descendants of Gad, and so forth (Numbers 1). To get an idea of the average size of each tribe, one can divide the total number of men counted by eleven, the number of tribes counted. The average tribe had 54,868 men. After 24,000 died in a plague, God told Moses to take another census. Then the average tribe had 54,703 men (Numbers 26).

These measures of central tendency summarize large amounts of data into one number whether we use the mean, as we did above, or the median or mode or some other measure of central tendency. They tell us what the "central" value is in some way.

Variability

Measures of variability tell us if the scores are all nearly the same or if they are quite different from each other. They tell us how much they are spread out--how "variable" they are. You are already familiar with one measure of variability--the range, which is the largest score minus the smallest. If the scores are all about the same, the range will be small. If the scores are quite different from each other, the range will be large.

When we looked at the average size of the tribes in the two censuses in Numbers, they were both about the same. We might conclude that not much had changed between the first and second census, but that would be the wrong conclusion.

The range in Numbers 1 was 39,200. That is, the largest tribe had 74,600 and the smallest had 35,400. The range in Numbers 26 was 63,000. The largest tribe had 85,200 and the smallest only 22,200. This tells us that the differences in the sizes of the tribes was greater after the plague than before it. In fact, the tribe of Simeon was larger than average in the first census, but the smallest of all in the second. Apparently the plague hit that tribe very hard.

Psychologists use not only the range, but such measures of variability as the standard deviation and the variance. All of these measures are smaller when the scores are similar and larger when the scores are markedly different.

Implications and Applications

Statistics can be misleading or used to mislead, especially if one does not understand what they mean. Psychologists widely use three measures of central tendency, the mean, the mode, and the median. Although all three tell us something about where the "center" is, they each mean something different. People who know what the differences are can choose the "average" that tells the story they want told.

Statisticians define each measure of central tendency slightly differently. The mean is the sum of all the scores divided by the number of scores. The median is the middle score. The mode is the score that occurs the most frequently. Thus each measure tells a slightly different story.

Let us take a simplified and exaggerated example. Suppose a pastor has to report the average attendance at his church for a month with five Sundays. He has 5 the first Sunday, 15 the second, 5 the third, 25 the fourth, and 5000 the fifth Sunday because of a Christian rock concert just down the road. What does he report for his average attendance?

If he has low self-esteem and wants to debase himself, he can correctly say that his average attendance for the month was five (the mode). If he is proud and haughty, he can just as correctly say that his average attendance for the month was over a thousand (the mean). Most statisticians would suggest using the median and saying that the average attendance was fifteen.

From our Christian perspective, we would ask psychologists to be honest in their use of statistics. In addition, we should understand what statistics mean and use them correctly ourselves.

References

Abbott, E. A. (1952). *Flatland.* New York: Dover. (Original work published 1884)

Adams, J. E. (1973). *The Christian counselor's manual.* Grand Rapids, MI: Baker.

Allport, G. W. (1955). *Becoming: Basic considerations for a psychology of personality.* New York: Yale University Press.

Allport, G. W. (1961). *Pattern and growth in personality.* New York: Holt, Rinehart and Winston.

Angoff, W. H. (1988). The nature-nurture debate, aptitudes, and group differences. *American Psychologist, 43,* 713-720.

Asch, S. (1955). Opinions and social pressure. *Scientific American, 193,* 31-35.

Bandura, A. (1971). *Social Learning Theory.* Morristown, NJ: General Learning Press.

Bandura, A. (1986). *Social foundations of thought and action: A social cognitive theory.* Englewood Cliffs, NJ: Prentice Hall.

Beck, A. T. (1976). *Cognitive therapy and the emotional disorders.* New York: International Universities Press.

Berkhof, L. (1946). *Systematic Theology.* Grand Rapids, MI: Eerdmans.

Bobgan, M., & Bobgan, D. (1987). *Psychoheresy.* Santa Barbara, CA: Eastgate.

Cannon, W. B. (1927). The James-Lange theory of emotion: A critical examination and an alternative theory. *American Journal of Psychology, 39,* 106-124.

Crooks R. L., & Stein, J. (1988). *Psychology: Science, behavior and life.* New York: Holt, Rinehart and Winston.

Darley, J., & Batson, D. (1973). "... From Jerusalem to Jericho"; A study of situation and dispositional variables in helping behavior. *Journal of Personality and Social Psychology, 27,* 100-108.

Dobson, J. (1970). *Dare to discipline.* Wheaton, IL: Tyndale.

Ellis, A. (1958). Rational psychotherapy. *Journal of General Psychology, 59,* 35-48.

Erikson, E. (1963). *Childhood and society* (2nd ed.). New York: Norton.

Eysenck H. J. (1952). The effects of psychotherapy: An evaluation. *Journal of Consulting Psychology, 16,* 319-324.

Fairlie, H. (1978). *The seven deadly sins today.* Washington, DC: New Republic.

Festinger, L. (1957). *A theory of cognitive dissonance.* Stanford, CA: Stanford University Press.

Freud, S. (1949). *An outline of psychoanalysis* (J. Strachey, Trans.). New York: Norton. (Original work published 1940)

Hilgard, E. R. (1986). *Divided Consciousness: Multiple controls on human thought and action.* New York: Wiley.

Hilgard, E. R., Atkinson, R. C., & Atkinson, R. L. (1975). *Introduction to psychology* (6th ed.). New York: Harcourt Brace Jovanovich.

Hubel, D. H., & Wiesel, T. N. (1979, September). Brain mechanisms of vision. *Scientific American,* 150-162.

Hunt, D., & McMahon, T. A. (1985). *The Seduction of Christianity.* Eugene, OR: Harvest House.

James, W. (1968). What is an emotion. In Arnold, M. B. (Ed.), *The nature of emotion.* Baltimore: Penguin. (Reprinted from *Mind,* 1884, *9,* 188-205).

Janis, I. (1972). *Victims of groupthink: A psychological study of foreign-policy decisions and fiascos.* Boston: Houghton Mifflin.

Joy, D. (1985). *Bonding: Relationships in the image of God.* Waco, TX: Word.

Kelly, G. A. (1955). *The psychology of personal constructs.* New York: Norton.

Kohlberg, L. (1973). Stages and aging in moral development--some speculations. *The Gerontologist, 13,* 497-502.

Kohler, W. (1959). *The mentality of apes* (E. Winter, Trans.). New York: Vintage. (Original work published 1925)

Kubler-Ross, E. (1975). *Death: The final stage of growth.* Englewood Cliffs, NJ: Prentice-Hall.

Leukel, F. (1976). *Introduction to physiological psychology* (3rd ed.). St. Louis: Mosby.

Lewis, C. S. (1970). The humanitarian theory of punishment. In W. Hooper (Ed.), *God in the dock.* Grand Rapids, MI: Eerdmans. (Reprinted from *20th Century: An Australian Quarterly Review, 3,* 1949.)

Limber, J. (1977). Language in child and chimp? *American Psychologist, 32,* 280-295.

Linn, D., & Linn, M. (1974). *Healing of memories.* Ramsey, NJ: Paulist.

Linn, R. (1982). Ability testing: Individual differences, prediction and differential prediction. In A. Wigder, & W. Gardner (Eds.), *Ability testing: Uses, consequences and controversies.* Washington, DC: National Academy Press.

Lorenz, K. (1966). *On Aggression.* (M. K. Wilson, Trans.). New York: Harcourt Brace Jovanovich. (Original work published 1963)

Maslow, A. H. (1954). *Motivation and personality.* New York: Harper & Row.

Maslow, A. H. (1964). *Religions, values, and peak-experiences.* New York: Viking.

Maslow, A. H. (1968). *Toward a psychology of being* (2nd ed.). New York: Van Nostrand.

Masters. W., & Johnson, V. (1975). *The pleasure bond: A new look at sexuality and commitment.* Boston: Little, Brown.

May, R. (1969). *Love and will.* New York: Norton.

McClelland, D. C. (1973). Testing for competence rather than for "intelligence." *American Psychologist, 28,* 1-14.

Meyer, S. G. (1975). Neuropsychology and worship. *Journal of Psychology and Theology, 3,* 281-289.

Milgram, S. (1963). Behavioral study of obedience. *Journal of Abnormal and Social Psychology, 67,* 231-246.

Moody, R. (1976). *Life after life.* Harrisburg, PA: Stackpole.

Morris, C. G. (1988). *Psychology: An introduction.* Englewood Cliffs, NJ: Prentice Hall.

Morris, D. (1971). *Intimate behavior.* New York: Bantam.

Myers, D. G. (1989). *Psychology* (2nd ed.). New York: Worth.

Pavlov, I. P. (1960). *Conditioned reflexes* (G. V. Anrep, Ed. and Trans.) New York: Dover. (Original work published 1927)

Piaget, J. (1973). *The child and reality.* New York: Grossman.

Rogers, C. (1959). A theory of therapy, personality, and interpersonal relationships, as developed in the client-centered framework. In S. Koch (Ed.) *Psychology: A study of a science* (Vol. 3). New York: McGraw-Hill.

Sall, M. J. (1976). Demon possession or psychopathology?: A clinical differentiation. *Journal of Psychology and Theology, 4,* 286-290.

Schachter, S., & Singer, J. E. (1962). Cognitive, social, and physiological determinants of emotional state. *Psychological Review, 69,* 379-399.

Schaeffer, F. A. (1968). *The God who is there.* Downers Grove, IL: Intervarsity.

Schur, M. (1972). *Freud: Living and Dying.* New York: International Universities Press.

Skinner, B. F. (1938). *The behavior of organisms.* New York: Appleton-Century-Crofts.

Smith, M. L., Glass, G. V., & Miller, R. L. (1980). *The benefits of psychotherapy.* Baltimore: Johns Hopkins.

Terrace, H. (1979, November). How Nim Chimsky changed my mind. *Psychology Today,* 63-91.

Tolman, E. C. (1932). *Purposive behavior in animals and men.* New York: Appleton-Century-Crofts.

Tozer, A. W. (1961). *The Knowledge of the holy.* New York: Harper & Brothers, 1961.

Wallace, R. K., & Benson, H. (1972). The physiology of meditation. *Scientific American, 227,* 84-90.

Watson, J. B. (1930). *Behaviorism* (rev. ed). Chicago: The University of Chicago press.

Watson, J. B. (1968). Psychology as the behaviorist views it. In W. S. Sahakian, (Ed.), *History of Psychology.* Itasca, IL: Peacock. (Reprinted from *Psychological Review,* 1913, *20*)

Index

Median, 105-106
Meditation, 39, 42
Memories, 37-38, 47, 56, 58-59
Memory, 17, 40, 55-61, 67, 73, 75, 79, 81, 85-86, 88, 91, 97
Memory aids, 59
Methods, 6-9, 11-13, 15, 19, 25, 31, 37, 43, 49, 53, 55, 60-61, 66-67, 73, 79-80, 85, 91-92, 97, 103-104
Meyer, S. G., 17
Milgram, S., 99, 101
Miller, R. L., 96
Mind, 17, 34, 51, 55-56, 80, 82, 103
MMPI, 81, 83
Mode, 105-106
Monocular cues, 32
Mood disorders, 86, 89
Moody, R., 40
Moral development, 20-21, 24
Morphemes, 50
Morris, C. G., 45
Morris, D., 98
Motivation, 11, 17, 61-68, 73, 77, 79, 81, 85-86, 88, 91, 97
Muller-Lyer illusion, 33-34
Muscles, 13, 15, 25, 28
Myers, D. G., 31
Narcissistic personality, 87
Near death experiences, 40
Nervous system, 14, 38, 41, 56, 63, 88
Neural pathway, 26-27
Neurons, 13-14, 17, 27, 32, 38, 62, 93
New Testament, 4, 35, 40-41, 90
Obedience, 99, 101
Observation, 8
Observational learning, 46
Obsessions, 93
Occult, 34
Old Testament, 28, 35, 40-41, 90
Operant conditioning, 44-47, 92
Operant conditioning therapies, 92
Original sin, 23, 77
Pain, 28, 40, 74, 88, 99

Paranoia, 81
Paranoid disorders, 86-87
Pavlov, I. P., 44
Peace, 71
Peak experiences, 71, 78
Perception, 10, 31-37, 43, 49, 55, 61-63, 67, 69, 72-73, 79, 81, 85, 86-88, 91, 97
Perfection, 53, 63, 75
Person-centered therapy, 94
Personality, 15, 22, 63, 73-83, 85-88, 91-94, 97
Personality disorders, 86-87
Phobias, 72
Phonemes, 50
Physiological psychology, 10, 13-15, 17, 31
Piaget, J., 20
Postconventional, 21
Prayer, 16, 34-35
Precognition, 35
Preconscious, 75
Preconventional, 21
Preoperational, 20
Pressure, 28, 42
Pride, 65
Privacy, 82
Problem solving, 51, 53
Projection, 35
Projective tests, 80
Prophecy, 35, 41
Psychoanalysis, 10, 11, 52, 74, 77, 95
Psychokinesis, 35
Psychosocial development, 22
Psychosurgery, 93
Psychotherapy, 36, 46, 53, 96
Punishment, 21-22, 24, 45-47, 76
Q-sort, 81
Range, 26-27, 105
Rational living, 53
Rationalization, 35
Reinforcement, 44-45, 74, 92
Religion, 1, 6, 39, 77, 101
Repentance, 18, 96